LIFE

to the Full

LIFE
to the Full

The Practical and
Powerful Writings of
James, Peter, John & Jude

DOUGLAS JACOBY

One Merrill Street
Woburn, Ma 01801
1-800-727-8273 FAX (617)937-3889

Life to the Full
©1995 by Discipleship Publications International
One Merrill Street, Woburn, MA 01801

Cover design and illustration: Chris Costello
Interior design: Anita Costello

Printed in the United States of America

ISBN 1-884553-71-0

To John Causey,
whose encouragement
inspired this book

Contents

Part III:
FROM DEATH TO LIFE

APPENDIXES

Introduction

Even Jesus Asked Questions

After three days they found him in the temple courts, sitting among the teachers, listening to them and asking them questions. Everyone who heard him was amazed at his understanding and his answers....
"Why were you searching for me?" he asked. "Didn't you know I had to be in my Father's house?" (Luke 2:46-47, 49).

Before delving into our intriguing study of James, Peter, John and Jude, we need some background information, as well as a background *attitude*. An inquiring mind appreciates helpful facts and background. So to begin with—this is so important!—*ask questions!* This is how all children learn, it's how Jesus learned the Scriptures, it's how the Ethiopian got started (Acts 8:34) and it's the only way we are going to learn too. A man or woman who really loves the word of God asks questions. To put it another way, in this case "the love that asks no questions" is not the love of God's word. A good student, like the only good Master, asks lots of questions!

Bloggs and Doe?

Really getting the message of James, Peter, John and Jude requires an understanding of (1) the author (his situation, personality, and even his writing style), (2) his audience (their situation and needs), (3) the time and circumstances of the letter and (4) the language in which the letter is written. Though all this sounds a bit technical, it applies even to understanding letters today. Before we read the letter John Doe in Boston sent to Joe Bloggs in London, there are some things we'd better understand.

For instance, who is John Doe (doctor, engineer, poet)? How have his life experiences affected his outlook and language? What do we make of his writing style? Exactly why is he writing to Joe Bloggs? Is this business correspondence or a letter to a family member? Is he initiating correspondence or replying to Bloggs' letter? Are we dropping into the middle of a series of letters? If the letter is written in English, we are probably okay. (Unless it was written three hundred years ago!) But what if it is in French or Japanese? Are we sure we have the translation right and that we understand the idioms and figures of speech?

New Testament (NT) scholars have to take all these factors into account. A casual attitude on the part of scholars could compromise the integrity of the translation or introduce foreign ideas into the text—in short, the word of God could be transformed into the word of man.

All this means there are a number of questions we need to constantly ask ourselves as we read through the Bible. Often we plow through the Bible asking few questions, making many assumptions, reading our opinions *into* the text ("eisegesis") rather than drawing the truths *out of* the text ("exegesis"). Do you want to take it higher? Are you ready to become a careful student of the Bible? Then, like Jesus, you need to ask questions!

Jesus asked questions. Mind-blowing! If he, the Son of God, carefully studied the Scriptures, how much more do we need to do our level best to "correctly handle" the word of truth?[1]

General Letters?

Why do we call them the "General Letters"? Are they vague and comfortable, whereas the letter to the Romans is specific? What does all this mean?

Scholars have come up with a name for the seven letters on which this practical commentary focuses—the "Catholic Epistles" or "General Letters." "Catholic" means "universal," translating the Greek *katholikos* from which the word comes. "Epistle" means "letter" from the Latin *epistula.*

Unlike the other letters of the NT, which are usually directed to specific communities, these seven are written to the church at large. If you want to sound brainy, call them the "Catholic Epistles" (at the risk of being misunderstood!). Oth-

---

[1]If you, the reader, want to take it higher, you will benefit enormously from Appendixes A and B. Perhaps this would be a good time to take a look at them; or maybe you'd like to read through the book first.

erwise, the term "General Letters" may find more favor! But call them what you will, these seven letters are the subject of this book.

Were Things Really That Different?

Something else to keep in mind is that life in the NT world was considerably different from life today. Forget this and you are likely to miss what, to the ancients, was obvious. Yes, man is essentially the same, and the Bible deals with the heart, but circumstances have changed radically. What were things like in the years 50-70 A.D.?

Powerful Roman "Caesars," or emperors, ruled the world. (A list of the earlier Caesars may be found in Appendix C on page 210.) Soldiers guarded the Roman empire and secured the provinces at the borders. Slavery was universal. Corruption was rampant, justice was in short supply. The international language was Greek—thanks to the influence of Alexander the Great some four centuries earlier. Judaism was still strong, the Temple was still standing, and "Judaizing" Christians (those who believed you could not be a Christian without keeping the Jewish law) were troubling the early church. Communication was completely different: no fax machines, digital communications systems, satellites or televisions—just writing. And even then, few people were able to read—much less write!—a letter.

So, to answer the question: Yes, things have changed tremendously in two thousand years! Don't forget it. This will help you get the most from God's word.

Can't I Just Take My Leaders' Word?

Do I have to study on my own? Why not just take the minister's word for it? And why study so intensively? Is all that hard work really necessary?

Well, as one convinced that every disciple has a personal responsibility to give 100% to master the Bible, let me reply. Why should we do our best in Bible study?
- God commands it! (Acts 17:11; Deuteronomy 17:19; Psalm 119:1-176)
- Jesus, our model, exemplified the type of inquiring mind that means so much to God.

- You can't borrow someone else's faith; you have to work out your *own* salvation. Watching someone else work out doesn't make you more fit!
- Studying gives potency and punch to your evangelism. Consistent study increases your competence, confidence and credibility with outsiders.
- Leaders can be wrong. No one has a monopoly on the truth; we all have things to learn. You may just discover something that will transform the kingdom of God! And even if leaders are teaching the truth, how they support it may be fallacious. "A proof text out of context is a pretext." In other words, methodology counts.
- One day you'll be a leader yourself! What kind of a leader are you going to be?

Why This Title?

"Life to the Full"? Isn't that a line borrowed from the gospel of John? So why use it here? Let me explain. Several words appear over and over again in the general letters, and "life" is one of those words. These men did not write to impress the scholars. They did not write to add to their résumés. They wrote because they had found life, and they wanted to pass it on. Of course it is not just mastering seven epistles that yields the abundant life. The entire word of God comes into play. Yet the life described and guaranteed in these dynamic and timeless letters is the very life of Jesus Christ. And because he lives forever, according to Hebrews 7:24, today we too can enjoy *life to the full.*

> *That which was from the beginning, which we have heard, which we have seen with our eyes, which we have looked at and our hands have touched—this we proclaim concerning the Word of life. The life appeared; we have seen it and testify to it, and we proclaim to you the eternal life, which was with the Father and has appeared to us (1 John 1:1-2).*

Doug Jacoby
London, September 1995

Part I

THE CROWN OF LIFE

JAMES

Blessed is the man who perseveres under trial, because when he has stood the test, he will receive the crown of life that God has promised to those who love him.

JAMES 1:12

There is only one way to obtain the crown of life: to pass the test with flying colors, as did the martyr James himself. His uncompromising message gives us the courage to do just that!

1

James: A Martyr's Message

INTRODUCTION

God has given us an incredibly practical letter in James. Virtually every verse in this hard-hitting epistle is both golden and memorable. Some scholars hold that James is a typical synagogue sermon, others that it is simply a normal letter to Jewish Christians. It contains numerous reflections of the Sermon on the Mount as well as echoes of extra-biblical Jewish literature. Before we begin, let's cover some background.

Political Background

To appreciate James and to see the logical flow of the letter, it is vital to understand the political background of Palestine at that time. These were troubled times: oppression under the Romans and those richer Jews who acted as their pawns, exorbitant taxes and food shortages, and with them, rioting and anti-Roman nationalistic fervor. Some landowners even hired thugs to execute or at least threaten tenants who were falling behind in their payments. The politically active Zealots, to whom Simon the Zealot, one of Jesus' apostles, had belonged (Matthew 10:4), urged the nation to revolt. This pressing combination of factors climaxed in the Jewish War of 66-73 A.D. In 70 A.D. Jerusalem and its temple were destroyed, never to be rebuilt. In 73 A.D. the fortress of Masada, which had held out longer than any other, fell with 1,000 Zealots committing suicide rather than be captured by the Romans.

If the history seems tangled, let's simplify: The rich were oppressing the poor. This is why James addresses the pride of the rich (1:9-11; 2:1-9, 13-17), persecution by the rich (2:6-7; 5:6) and economic exploitation by the rich (5:4-6). Patient endurance, not violent retaliation, is enjoined upon the Christians. Without this perspective, the letter of James is difficult to appreciate and to understand.

Religious Background

James appears to have been written to *Jewish* Christians—Christians familiar with the Jewish Law (what we call the Old Testament) and who were following it to some extent and were proud of their religious roots. He writes to the "twelve tribes" (1:1). This did not indicate that all the tribes were necessarily intact, but was most likely a way of identifying their Hebrew heritage.

James mentions the synagogue ("meeting," NIV) in 2:2. Abraham is "our ancestor" in 2:21. There are several references to the Old Testament (OT) (5:10, 11, 17), as well as allusions like those in 1:25 ("perfect law") and 2:8 ("royal law"). The elders in 5:14 may have been Jewish elders before their conversion.[1]

The "twelve tribes" of the dispersion (James uses the word "scattered") points back to the captivities suffered by the Jews during the Assyrian and Babylonian periods (8th-6th centuries B.C.). Remember, these are Jewish Christians to whom James is writing. The continual peril faced by the twelve tribes was not so much *annihilation* as *assimilation*. Assimilation of morality and spirituality to the low levels of paganism and ultimate absorption into the mainstream of heathenism. (Read all about it in 2 Kings 17.) The constant temptation to compromise cost most of the sons of Jacob their salvation, as the OT makes very clear. For Christians scattered throughout a heathen world, the goal is to remain *in* the world without becoming *of* the world!

Personal Background

Matthew names James as one of Jesus' four brothers, as well as mentioning "all his sisters" (Matthew 13:55-56). Though

---

[1] The lack of mention of circumcision may seem odd, considering its prominence in Romans, Galatians and other letters directed towards churches with a substantial number of Jewish members. But circumcision was really not an issue in Israel or among purely Jewish communities. The most controversial issue in the first-century church, as you may know, was the Jew-Gentile controversy: Must Gentiles become Jews before they become Christians or exactly how much of the Law carries over into the NT? To put it simply, circumcision sometimes became a huge issue *outside Israel* as disciples with a Jewish background interacted with those who were Gentiles (Acts 15, Galatians, Romans 4, Philippians 3), but it was a non-issue *in Israel* among those who shared the Jewish heritage. James is not writing to people unfamiliar with the Law. Surprisingly to some of us, Jewish Christians observed the Law and often zealously (Acts 21:20).

James was Jesus' junior, he was the eldest of the eight or nine siblings. The brothers are all named, but in keeping with usual Jewish custom, the women are unnamed (Genesis 5, etc.). Thus James and Jesus (surprisingly) came from a family of at least ten!

In the NT, James is by far the most significant (half-)brother of Jesus (Matthew 13:55, Mark 6:3, Acts 1:14). Joseph, James' father, seems to have died by the time Jesus began his ministry. James was related to Elizabeth and a cousin of John the Baptist—related through Elizabeth (Luke 1:36). Of James' other brothers, Judas (Jude) is the most significant (Matthew 13:55, Jude 1:1).

What happened to Joseph (the father), of whom we hear nothing after Luke 2? And, a related question, why did Jesus wait so long (till age 32 or so) before beginning his public ministry? Was Joseph dead? He is never mentioned in the latter portions of the gospels. Since, in those days, women married a little younger than men, Mary may well have outlived Joseph. Jesus' instructions in John 19 would have been strange if Joseph were still alive.

As eldest brother, Jesus would have had many responsibilities, not just in running the family business (Joseph was a carpenter or some other kind of craftsman, according to the Greek text) but especially to his siblings and mother. It is reasonable to guess that Jesus would have waited until the number two son (James) was ready to meet the needs of his mother and the other six to eight children before launching his career. In working the family business, Jesus was becoming more "relatable" as our Savior and model (Hebrews 4:15, 5:7-9), since most people have *jobs* and *family commitments*. His working experience certainly gave him credibility with older men, people in general, detractors—everybody. So considering Jesus' (first) coming came after thousands of years of human history, an extra 32 years was no big deal. Patience!

James' Conversion

Jesus loved his family enough to take a stand for the kingdom of God. We see early in the gospel of Mark that Mary and her sons did not appreciate Jesus' identity and mission (Mark 3:20-21, 31). They would not go into the meeting; instead they sent a messenger to fetch Jesus, whom they think has gone over the top! James and the other brothers are Jesus' would-be advisers in John 7:1-5. But Jesus' teaching about family was always clear, not only in Luke 2:46-51, but also in Matthew 10:34-39 and other passages of instruction to disciples: God first and family second. (Disciples, how much have you taken a stand with *your* family?)

Surely we must conclude that Jesus' love played a key role in winning over James and the rest of the family. Even on the cross, Jesus' selfless devotion was demonstrated (John 19:26-27). As a result of this and the power of his resurrection, by Acts 1:14, Jesus' physical family, including James and Jude, was part of the nucleus of believers. Jesus' refusal to compromise paid off after a few years. We, too, are in the Christian life for the long haul. Do you have the patience to wait years, if necessary, to win over those whom you love? James was the direct beneficiary of Jesus' love and unwavering commitment to the truth—even over his own blood relationships.

Simply put, the great James was *converted* because Jesus refused to be *diverted*.

Career and Writing

It must be made clear that James was not the apostle James, son of Zebedee (Acts 12:2). He did, however, become the leader of the Jerusalem church, replacing Peter, probably due to Peter's responsibilities outside Jerusalem (see Acts 12:17, 15:13, 21:18, Galatians 1:19, 2:9, 12), and left us with the epistle of James (James 1:1). Galatians 1:19 possibly indicates he was recognized as an apostle. According to Josephus, the Jewish historian, James was stoned to death by the Jews in 62 A.D.

Certainly if Jesus and his brothers had left us with more writings, many of our questions about the Messiah's family would be answered (not that they need to be answered for our faith to be complete!), yet the legacy of writing is a rather short list:

- James: He left us with his compact and compelling letter, James.
- Jude: His contribution was the colorful and uncompromising letter of Jude.
- Jesus: He left us with nothing by his own hand. (And yet everything, as the incarnate Word!)

Date of James

The consensus of scholars is that James was written about 48 A.D. If this is the case, it predates 1 Thessalonians (about 50 A.D.) and Galatians (about 49 A.D.), and thus is the oldest NT letter—probably the oldest NT document.

The Martyr's Message

James was a man of God. "Old Camel Knees," according to tradition, knew his Lord not just as a physical brother, but as the risen Savior. His message promises to hit our hearts, too— where it hurts and so that we can change. Let's open our hearts, minds and Bibles and get ready to learn from the martyr's message.

? Think what it must have been like to have been a brother of Jesus. How would it have affected you? What thoughts would you have had when you realized how much you had misunderstood him? How would the resurrection have affected you? What kind of heart must James have had to have earned the name "Old Camel Knees"?

2

A Crown, Not a Frown
JAMES 1

Why does James cut the heart of every man and woman who reads it? Why do so many feel that this letter is so down-to-earth and readable? James is so practical because it addresses Christians under pressure, and aren't we all under pressure? Medical professionals tell us that without pressure and stress, the human body soon slows down and dies. Pressure keeps the blood flowing, the adrenaline surging and the character changing.

> *¹James, a servant of God and of the Lord Jesus Christ,*
> *To the twelve tribes scattered among the nations: Greetings.*

James calls himself in this passage, not the *brother*, but the *servant* of the Lord Jesus Christ. Even though he was a most prominent leader in the early church—Peter's successor in the leadership of the great Jerusalem church—he kept a humble disposition and a down-to-earth perspective. Anyone in a leadership role needs the same attitude. We are here to *serve.*

The "twelve tribes" mostly likely refers to Jewish Christians. They are scattered among the heathen. The question: to succumb and compromise, or stay strong and remain faithful—a question confronting every Christian everywhere every day.

> *²Consider it pure joy, my brothers, whenever you face trials of many kinds, ³because you know that the testing of your faith develops perseverance. ⁴Perseverance must finish its work so that you may be mature and complete, not lacking anything. ⁵If any of you lacks wisdom, he should ask God, who gives generously to all without finding fault, and it will be given to him. ⁶But when he asks, he must believe and not doubt, be-*

cause he who doubts is like a wave of the sea, blown and tossed by the wind. [7]That man should not think he will receive anything from the Lord; [8]he is a double-minded man, unstable in all he does.

How are trials to be met? Trials such as poverty and oppression by the rich, as in the situation of James, or other testing situations? Pure joy. This is hardly our natural reaction when we face trials of *any* kind at all! But God is at work. Romans 5:1-5 amplifies the thought. Christian joy isn't the blithe, naive grin of the traditional "Christian," insulated and self-focused; rather it's something deeply embedded in the heart of a committed disciple on the radical edge, like James who met hardship with prayer, earning his reputation as "Old Camel Knees."

Perseverance must finish its work. There are only two options: we continue in the process of becoming mature and complete or we fall away. That is blunt, but it's the truth. The flesh shuns hard work and discipline. (So does the "fool," according to the book of Proverbs.) The Christian life requires tremendous discipline! Maturity isn't just spiritual longevity; it's shown in how you react to pressure. For further thought, scan Proverbs, and then see Hebrews 12. For extrabiblical reading, I recommend both Richard Taylor's *The Disciplined Life* and Oswald Sanders' *Spiritual Leadership*.

If we lack wisdom, according to James, all we need to do is ask for it. God *wants* to bless us. Now "wisdom" doesn't mean intellectual knowledge or high IQ. Rather, it is something spiritual—knowing what to do in tricky situations. It is not likely God will make you more intelligent than you already are, but it's a promise of God that he will enable you to *live* more intelligently! James assures us that this kind of wisdom can be attained through prayer. Any disciple has the capacity to become "wise beyond his years" by becoming a diligent student of the Scriptures and human behavior, then testing what he has learned in daily life. That's possible only through prayer and dependence on God.

? What was the last big trial that you faced? How did you respond? Did you let God disciple you, or did you resist, complain or even retaliate?

⁹The brother in humble circumstances ought to take pride in his high position. ¹⁰But the one who is rich should take pride in his low position, because he will pass away like a wild flower. ¹¹For the sun rises with scorching heat and withers the plant; its blossom falls and its beauty is destroyed. In the same way, the rich man will fade away even while he goes about his business.

James puts the material world in perspective. Poor people can be saved, and so can rich people (see 1 Timothy 6:17-19), but both need to watch their step. Two biblical books which focus extensively on the theme of wealth are Proverbs and Luke, each of which has more than thirty verses on the use and misuse of money. See for example Proverbs 30:7-9, which teaches a middle way between poverty and riches because each has its own dangers.[1]

¹²Blessed is the man who perseveres under trial, because when he has stood the test, he will receive the crown of life that God has promised to those who love him. ¹³When tempted, no one should say, "God is tempting me." For God cannot be tempted by evil, nor does he tempt anyone; ¹⁴but each one is tempted when, by his own evil desire, he is dragged away and enticed. ¹⁵Then, after desire has conceived, it gives birth to sin; and sin, when it is full-grown, gives birth to death.

If we keep our head and our faith, and keep away from the perils of materialism, we will one day receive the "crown of life." This crown is received neither quickly nor cheaply. The price is high; the reward is infinite. We can persevere under trial, or we can frown and get a bad attitude. The attitude may be directed towards any human individual, or it may be against God. Yet we should never blame God. He is always fair. We take it as axiomatic that God is both good and fair, and we should sooner doubt our own existence than doubt the basic justice and goodness of God.

Disciples the world over have used (but never benefited from) these rationalizations:

---

[1] For further reading on the Christian and economics, see R. J. Sider, *Rich Christians Living in an Age of Hunger.*

- My upbringing was less than perfect.
- Someone dropped me on my head when I was a child.
- I'm different; I need lots of sleep.
- Life is so busy.
- I'm just a young Christian, please excuse me.
- I'm an older Christian, please excuse me.
- No one understands me; I'm a special case.
- My DNA is messed up, but hopefully the Genome Project will save me.
- I just don't hear my alarm clock in the morning!
- I used to be a lot worse.
- The children need their sleep, so I cannot come.
- Jesus said "daily," but he didn't say *how many times* a day (Luke 9:23).

If you are more dependent on these explanations than you are on God, you will always find a reason why you cannot persevere. But if you are convinced God loves you and will help you find a way, you will overcome the odds and move through trial after trial.

James likens the process of temptation to biological growth: conception, pregnancy, delivery, growth and maturity. Desire itself is not sin; sinful desire cherished, however, is lust. As Martin Luther was fond of saying, "You can't stop a bird from flying over your head, but you can keep him from building a nest in your hair"! We are not *victims,* and by God's power we can be *victors!*

? Do you take responsibility when under pressure, or would you like some handy excuses? Is your tendency to look for someone else to blame, or do you own up to your own failures, mistakes and sins?

> [16]*Don't be deceived, my dear brothers.* [17]*Every good and perfect gift is from above, coming down from the Father of the heavenly lights, who does not change like shifting shadows.* [18]*He chose to give us birth through the word of truth, that we might be a kind of firstfruits of all he created.*

God is in control! God doesn't work in our lives (through testing) to *ruin* us, but to *improve* us. Follow the example of Job; don't accuse God of wrongdoing (Job 1:22). The "heavenly lights" in Jewish literature are the stars. Astrology was

popular in James' time, as it is today. The good news is that
God is in control; the astrologers are dead wrong! Our fate is
in God's living hands, not in the stars, so keep yourself close
to him.

One example of God's goodness is his gift of rebirth. He
gave us rebirth through obedience to the word of truth. As
Peter makes clear (1 Peter 1:23) this occurs in baptism (1 Peter
1:3, 23, 3:21). No one can be saved apart from submission to
the will of God as revealed in the word of God.

> [19]*My dear brothers, take note of this: Everyone should be
> quick to listen, slow to speak and slow to become angry,* [20]*for
> man's anger does not bring about the righteous life that God
> desires.* [21]*Therefore, get rid of all moral filth and the evil that
> is so prevalent and humbly accept the word planted in you,
> which can save you.*

James' message is clear here: Don't retaliate when times
are tough. In the world, the adage would read: "Be slow to
listen, quick to speak and quick to become angry—it's your
right!" But Jesus *and* James taught that ego must be crucified,
be self-controlled. James' wisdom would transform many a
relationship, if only it were put into practice. People retaliate
in several ways: fits of rage, membership in a reactionary group,
antisocial behavior or prejudging others and interpreting any
attempt at explanation as unreasonable.

? Do you receive the word of God humbly? With the attitude of 1 Thessalonians
2:13? What evidence is there that this is your attitude? Why is this attitude so right
and so powerful? Do you expect those you are sharing the Bible with to have the
same attitude?

> [22]*Do not merely listen to the word, and so deceive your-
> selves. Do what it says.* [23]*Anyone who listens to the word but
> does not do what it says is like a man who looks at his face in
> a mirror* [24]*and, after looking at himself, goes away and imme-
> diately forgets what he looks like.* [25]*But the man who looks
> intently into the perfect law that gives freedom, and continues
> to do this, not forgetting what he has heard, but doing it—he
> will be blessed in what he does.*

True freedom is not *political* freedom, but *spiritual* freedom! Remember from your reading of the gospels (John 6:15) how avidly the Jews sought political freedom? But the Zealots of James' time were mistaken, as are the Marxists, Anarchists and Liberation Theologians of our generation. Do we gaze into that perfect law (God's word as in Psalm 119) and refuse to look away? When we do, God blesses us and we experience an awesome freedom. When we don't, God opposes us and life becomes a burden. How do you feel about your spiritual life? Your answer is directly related to your relationship with God.

> ²⁶*If anyone considers himself religious and yet does not keep a tight rein on his tongue, he deceives himself and his religion is worthless.* ²⁷*Religion that God our Father accepts as pure and faultless is this: to look after orphans and widows in their distress and to keep oneself from being polluted by the world.*

Religion without self-control is useless, a common biblical theme. This verse is useful for your churchgoing friends who, true to their worldly nature, still use their tongues for gossip, slander, cursing, swearing, flattery and deceit. But 2:26 is also useful for disciples. (If you are convicted, skim the Proverbs and find dozens of verses on the right and wrong use of the tongue.)

True religion has a strong backbone of morality. Lack of social concern is a sure sign that a person is a false Christian. Worldly values and social apathy go hand in hand. See the scathing denunciation of Judah in Ezekiel 16:49. Do we really care about the needy and the disadvantaged, the "orphans and widows" of our day? True disciples ought to be eagerly "helping other people everywhere." Here are some suggestions:

- Pray about adopting a child. Don't allow selfishness to hold you back.
- Spend time with the bereaved. Visit a nursing home.
- Don't be stingy; when the homeless ask for spare change; give it to them (Luke 6:30-38).
- Volunteer quickly when church leaders ask for workers to support various programs. Your reward will be in heaven.

- For your next vacation, visit the Third World. Keep your eyes and heart open.
- Discuss with your friends what you can sell and use to help the poor (Luke 12:33).
- Get to know a homeless person and have such a person into your home (Matthew 25:35).
- Read the newspapers and follow up on victims of robbery, fires, accidents, etc. We are the light of the world!
- Get advice in all these areas. Be wise, but find ways to show compassion.

Do you want to wear that crown? Then when pressures come, don't frown. Determine to be part of solution. (Don't remain part of the problem.) The martyr's message of living faith continues. On to James 2!

? Do you ever doubt that the word of God is "the perfect law that gives freedom"? What causes such doubts? Do you know of anything that works as well in people's lives as the word of God? What ideas in the list above regarding pure religion most challenge you?

3

Dead or Alive?
JAMES 2

Dead or alive: How would God describe *your* faith, *your* life of discipleship? Religious people (the term isn't necessarily complimentary) usually betray their shallow faith and commitment by the unloving way they treat their fellow man. Sinful attitudes, sparse evangelism, superficial conversations, aloofness from true disciples, a lack of confession: These are the sure marks of a dead faith. Yes, there is some outward form of belief (2 Timothy 3:5), but the faith has no pulse. It is from such dangers that James the martyr seeks to protect the community; for it is better to die with a living faith than to live with a dead faith.

> *¹My brothers, as believers in our glorious Lord Jesus Christ, don't show favoritism. ²Suppose a man comes into your meeting wearing a gold ring and fine clothes, and a poor man in shabby clothes also comes in. ³If you show special attention to the man wearing fine clothes and say, "Here's a good seat for you," but say to the poor man, "You stand there" or "Sit on the floor by my feet," ⁴have you not discriminated among yourselves and become judges with evil thoughts?*

Favoritism shows itself in courts of law, in social settings and even in church. James mentions the well-dressed dude who enters an assembly (the Greek word here is *sunagog*e) and receives undue attention. When we show favoritism we are unlike God. Instead of being judges with good thoughts, we are judges with evil thoughts. This was the problem James addressed. It is a manifestation of the spirit of the world, ever crouching at the door of the Christian church.

? When are you most tempted to discriminate or show favoritism? Why does this run so counter to the gospel? Are there any ways in which you show greater respect to the more "high profile" disciples than to the "weaker members" who need it even more?

Excursus: "Judging"

Though it's often remarked that we should not "judge," this is a serious oversimplification of matters. Judging itself is merely drawing a conclusion based on evidence, premises or propositions. In the Scriptures there are at least ten or twelve different types of judging, and certain kinds of judging are prohibited or discouraged including:
- Hypocritical judging (Matthew 7:1-5; Romans 2:1)
- Superficial judging (John 7:24)
- Judgment in disputable matters (Romans 14:1; Colossians 2:16)
- Analyzing another's motives (1 Corinthians 4:3-5)
- Judging someone to be inferior to you or your group (James 1:3-4)
- Grumbling against a brother (James 5:9)

Other types of judging are definitely encouraged:
- Judging whether someone is receptive (Matthew 7:6)
- Coming to a *correct* conclusion (Luke 12:57)
- Spiritual judgments (1 Corinthians 2:15)
- Church discipline (1 Corinthians 5:12-13)
- Adjudicating in litigation (1 Corinthians 6:5)
- Being convicted by spiritual worship (1 Corinthians 14:25)

And then some types of judgment belong to God alone:
- Judgment regarding retribution (Hebrews 10:30)
- Final judgment (John 12:48; 1 Peter 4:5)

> *[5]Listen, my dear brothers: Has not God chosen those who are poor in the eyes of the world to be rich in faith and to inherit the kingdom he promised those who love him? [6]But you have insulted the poor. Is it not the rich who are exploiting you? Are they not the ones who are dragging you into court? [7]Are they not the ones who are slandering the noble name of him to whom you belong?*

The rich were the opponents of the Christians, and they manipulated the law courts to their own ends. In fact, Roman law favored the rich: persons of lower class could not sue persons of a higher class; and moreover, penalties were stricter for those of common birth than for the aristocrats. Is it necessary to remind the reader that in most of the world the situation is little changed today? "Money talks."

Hebrew law, in stark contrast, is no respecter of persons. The careful reader will marvel at the all-pervading sense of justice in the Pentateuch (the first five books of the OT). God is just, his laws are just, and this should give us great confidence.

Of course God's justice does not guarantee life will be fair, though *ultimately* all wrongs will be righted. In fact James himself was executed in 62 A.D., the year Festus (Acts 24-26) died, at the hands of the high priest Ananus II. (As in the vein of the book of James, he had been preaching against the rich Jews who were exploiting their brothers.) When James was stoned, the public outcry was tremendous! Indeed James the Just, as he was also called, had many friends in Israel.[1]

> [8]*If you really keep the royal law found in Scripture, "Love your neighbor as yourself," you are doing right. [9]But if you show favoritism, you sin and are convicted by the law as lawbreakers. [10]For whoever keeps the whole law and yet stumbles at just one point is guilty of breaking all of it. [11]For he who said, "Do not commit adultery," also said, "Do not murder." If you do not commit adultery but do commit murder, you have become a lawbreaker.*
>
> [12]*Speak and act as those who are going to be judged by the law that gives freedom, [13]because judgment without mercy will be shown to anyone who has not been merciful. Mercy triumphs over judgment!*

James urges certain of his brothers not to retaliate and others not to side with the exploiters (2:8-13). These Christians were tempted to be unmerciful. (There is a difference between compassion and softness.) In a fundamentally unjust and corrupt society, these are the temptations: revolution or compromise, retaliation or connivance, reaction or corruption.

"The royal law," which supersedes any law of man (just or unjust) demands that we love our neighbor (Leviticus 19:18), no matter who he is or what he may be doing to us. The law is royal because it is the law of our *true* sovereign, Jesus Christ. It

---

[1] Craig S. Keener, editor, *The IVP Bible Background Commentary*, (Downers Grove, Illinois: Inter-Varsity Press), 1993, p. 687.

is seldom, if ever, observed outside Jesus Christ and his body on earth, the church of Jesus Christ. Even true disciples will admit the difficulty of observing it.

Now ask the man in the street what the most important part of the Bible is and chances are he will say, "The Ten Commandments." And he would be wrong! The top two commandments are to love God wholeheartedly (Deuteronomy 6:5) and to love your neighbor as yourself (Leviticus 19:18). Jesus says explicitly that these are the two most important commands (Matthew 22:34-40). Interestingly, *neither* is in the Decalogue (the Ten Commandments).

What is the mark of true Christianity? Adherence to these two laws with both now viewed through the cross of Christ. That means *total commitment* and *total involvement*. Commitment to God as his disciples and involvement with both the saved and the lost in fellowship and evangelism, respectively. As long as we keep these two commands at the top of our priority list, our emphasis will be neither warped nor unbiblical.

A Few Comments on Retaliation

People are searching for a cause. Unfortunately, ignoring the royal law, which forbids us to act out of anger or to slander our neighbor, many people get involved in reactionary groups. For example, while the feminist movement has some good points to make, it is fundamentally a movement fueled by resentment. Human rights and women's rights are great things, but when the horizons of a person's thinking are dominated by worldly thinking (i.e. "I want *my* rights, and I want them *now!*"), this is not "the wisdom that comes from heaven" (see James 3:17).

Environmental concern is a Christian responsibility, but would you consider it legitimate to forcibly oppose those who disagree? From a biblical viewpoint, while nature and environment are delicately balanced and man is charged to exercise responsible "dominion" over them (Genesis 1:26), they are not the end-all of existence, and only a materialist could think they were. There are other more important causes!

Animal rights—yes! (Proverbs 12:10)—but human rights *are* more important! Many folks are far more concerned with the fate of whales, birds and insects than they are with their literal next-door neighbors. This is not the royal law. Again, this is not to say Christians may not be concerned about these areas, but if such causes are more important to you than human concern, fellowship and evangelism, your priorities are seriously out of balance and not Christlike.

The Gay Rights Movement is primarily a defensive and reactionary movement, whose members are, as a whole, far, far from "gay." It's hard to be happy or fulfilled when your cause is a *negative* one. The problem is not just that homosexuality is sinful (Romans 1), but the movement as a whole lacks goodwill, charity and love, the emphasis being self-justification rather than justification with God through Jesus Christ.

Opinion differs among believers about the extent to which political involvement is appropriate, but one thing is certain: when our political allegiance eclipses our Christian allegiance, we are in sin![2]

Anti-abortion protesters make some most important points: The fetus is alive, and life has a God-given sanctity. Psalm 139 and other passages make this clear. But who authorized anyone to attack, or even kill, a physician who performs abortions? Is this the way of Jesus Christ? Vote, yes; share your convictions with your friends, yes; but force is most emphatically *not* the way of God! These and many other movements of man do not fulfill the royal law of God (love for neighbor). They are more often than not fueled by hatred and self-interest. They seldom, if ever, appeal to the Bible for support and always minimize the sovereignty of God and his claim to our total allegiance. They reinforce a warped and man-centered world view and must be seen as such by all Bible-believing persons.

? How does "mercy triumph over judgment" in the way in which you relate to other people? Are there examples when the opposite occurs? How does the gospel of Jesus go deeper than many well-publicized social movements?

> [14]*What good is it, my brothers, if a man claims to have faith but has no deeds? Can such faith save him?* [15]*Suppose a brother or sister is without clothes and daily food.* [16]*If one of you says*

---

[2] Whatever your view of politics, failing to support your political leaders from the heart (1 Timothy 2; 1 Peter 2; Romans 13) is also sin and must be rejected by true Christians. The only exception to this is when leaders are calling on you to disobey God (Acts 5:29).

to him, "Go, I wish you well; keep warm and well fed," but does nothing about his physical needs, what good is it? [17]In the same way, faith by itself, if it is not accompanied by action, is dead.

This passage is well-known to all Christians, and in it James stresses that a saving faith is a working faith. Unfortunately many exegetes, including Martin Luther (16th century), have misunderstood James' words and supposed they contradicted the teaching of Paul on grace and works. At one point Luther called James an "epistle of straw" not worthy of a place in the NT. (Luther also excluded Jude, Hebrews and Revelation).

Notice James' emphasis on social action and practical charity. A Christian who has no interest in helping the disadvantaged is no Christian at all, for Jesus was the one who saw the crowds and had compassion on them and healed their sick (Matthew 14:14). He was the one who taught that only those who had reached out to the poor, the sick, the hungry and the imprisoned would be welcomed into heaven (Matthew 25:31-46).

[18]But someone will say, "You have faith; I have deeds. Show me your faith without deeds, and I will show you my faith by what I do."

"Nice" non-Christians often contrast the good done by unbelievers with the apathy of most denominations. It's true: such faith—tepid, lifeless, vague—is just as bad as unbelief. Don't many unbelievers make *some* efforts to change the world? James recognizes the common allegation against Christians and shames us with it.

[19]You believe that there is one God. Good! Even the demons believe that—and shudder.
[20]You foolish man, do you want evidence that faith without deeds is useless?

Mere belief is not enough. Read Titus 1:15, and ask yourself whether these people believe or not. Then read Titus 1:16, and get ready for the shock. You see, technically, anyone who isn't a true disciple is an "unbeliever." Our terminology ought to reflect that fact. In short, what good is it to wear "A face that you keep in a jar by the door? Who is it for?"

> *21Was not our ancestor Abraham considered righteous for what he did when he offered his son Isaac on the altar? 22You see that his faith and his actions were working together, and his faith was made complete by what he did. 23And the scripture was fulfilled that says, "Abraham believed God, and it was credited to him as righteousness," and he was called God's friend.*

True faith must be integrated with deeds. Someone who wants to dispute this, defending himself from the truth, is not worthy of Jesus. And when people like this, unwilling to change, "get saved," it brings reproach on Christ. All day long the name of God is blasphemed, thanks to the lukewarmness of so-called Christians. Their faith is dead, not alive.

> *24You see that a person is justified by what he does and not by faith alone.*

This is the verse that many churchgoers cannot believe is in the Bible! James isn't actually talking about the *point* of initial salvation, but rather, the lifestyle of the saved person. There is only one standard; it does not become more difficult once we are baptized. We are saved by a living faith, and we will stay saved by a living faith. The heirs of Martin Luther declare we are saved by *faith alone*, but true living faith is never alone. It is always accompanied by a heart that obeys.

> *25In the same way, was not even Rahab the prostitute considered righteous for what she did when she gave lodging to the spies and sent them off in a different direction? 26As the body without the spirit is dead, so faith without deeds is dead.*

James takes the example of the harlot Rahab, familiar to his audience (see Joshua 2). Even a prostitute puts the inactive religious person to shame! Echoes of Jesus' ministry: The prostitutes and tax collectors were entering the kingdom of heaven ahead of the Pharisees.

James leaves us with a pithy illustration. *Deeds* are what animate faith just as the spirit is what makes the body alive. Jesus spoke often of deeds, seldom of intentions (Matthew 7:21-23). Even in Revelation, where forty years after his resurrection he gave sermons to the churches of Asia, Jesus constantly focuses on deeds (Revelation 2:2, 19; 3:1, 8, 15). "Show me a faith that is alone—without deeds," James would say, "and I will show you a faith that is as useless as it is dead."

So is your faith *dead* or *alive?* Even if you don't know, God does; and through James he helps us not only to see clearly, but also to get back on track!

? What deeds in your life show that your faith is alive and well? Do you have any tendency to excuse yourself because, after all, salvation is by grace? What deeds of faith are most needed in your life right now?

4

Two Kinds of Wisdom
JAMES 3

As faith may be dead or alive, so "wisdom" can be earthly or heavenly, demonic or divine. The problem with the wrong sort of religion is that it's sparked by wrong attitudes and motives. The heart must be dealt with, and according to Jesus, there is a direct link between the heart and the mouth (Luke 6:45). What is said and how it is said—the matter of the *tongue*—is the subject of the third chapter of James.

> *¹Not many of you should presume to be teachers, my brothers, because you know that we who teach will be judged more strictly. ²We all stumble in many ways. If anyone is never at fault in what he says, he is a perfect man, able to keep his whole body in check.*

Is James referring to *false* teachers who claimed it was "wiser" to resist the aristocrats and Roman overlords through violent, revolutionary activity? The danger with the wrong type of teacher is his misuse of his tongue and the way this can influence others. Sarcasm, negativity, bitterness and cursing are natural and worldly reactions in a time of oppression, yet they are never appropriate for one who claims to be a disciple of Jesus!

Probably James' warning can be extended to *all* teachers and speakers. Certainly there is no one on earth who isn't deeply challenged when reading James 3. Coming across self-righteously is a danger we all face in our teaching, evangelism, counseling and even our fellowship. James, though he was the leader of the movement in Palestine, does not hesitate to include himself in the category of those who "stumble in many ways." We all appreciate humility in our leaders.

Excursus: Teachers

In religious circles the biblical role of "teacher" has received little attention, apart from the stagnant cloisters of Christian academia. Elders, preachers and others have held the limelight. Yet, in fact, teaching is one of the few gifts mentioned both in the lists of Ephesians 4 and 1 Corinthians 12, and in light of James 3:1 and other passages, one that doesn't seem to have passed away with the completed revelation of the New Testament. You may have noticed that Acts 13:1 says, "In the church at Antioch there were prophets and teachers: Barnabas, Simeon called Niger, Lucius of Cyrene, Manaen (who had been brought up with Herod the tetrarch) and Saul." These men were not mere academics in ivory towers, but dynamic gospel preachers who sought to teach the Scriptures to their generation in a powerful, pertinent and persuasive way. Many brothers today are interested in becoming teachers—a healthy development—but what exactly *is* a teacher?

- Though *exactly* what it is remains undefined, their primary job, as seen in the Bible, was to teach the Scriptures, like Ezra in the post-exilic times of the 5th century B.C. False prophets promulgated false teaching in NT times just as in OT times (Compare 2 Peter 2:1 and Jeremiah 8:7-8), so to keep on the straight and narrow, we need teachers of the truth (Matthew 7:13-15). Teachers are needed to set in order and arrange biblical themes (Ecclesiastes 12:9-10). When they do this poignantly, the movement of God will be "firmly embedded" because for Christians, Bible teachings are "firmly embedded nails" (Ecclesiastes 12:11).
- So what's the difference between teachers and preachers? The same as the difference between teaching and preaching: the former is primarily *instructional* while the latter is primarily *inspirational*. In the case of the men referred to in Acts 13, they combined both roles (as prophets *and* teachers); yet there is no reason that preaching and teaching gifts would always have to be combined in the same person.
- Teachers must be men of deep conviction. Allowing people without deep convictions to teach the disciples is positively *dangerous!* You who aspire to be teachers, how solid is your faith and how deep are your convictions? Do you readily

inspire, persuade and motivate others through your working knowledge of the Bible?

- Few Christians have the gift of teaching, and, although teaching the gospel is a command for all disciples, still only a few should aspire to be teachers in the more specialized sense of the word. Some evangelists are also excellent teachers, though not as many have enough of an academic grasp of the Scriptures to really qualify as teachers.

- Finally, teachers have got to be on the cutting edge! Because when teachers are not at their best spiritually, their teaching (both ideas and emphases) becomes affected. But when teachers are growing in their walk with the Lord and living effective, fruitful Christian lives, their words have power and their instruction has punch. The traditional seminary approach, with its unbalanced emphasis on academics, has some serious pitfalls. On the other hand, we cannot afford to ignore careful (even painstaking) exegesis, learning the original languages and digging deeply into the many lessons of history. Putting it all together, if the church is going to *be* God's cutting edge, all elders, evangelists and teachers are going to need to keep themselves daily on the cutting edge.

> [13]When we put bits into the mouths of horses to make them obey us, we can turn the whole animal. [4]Or take ships as an example. Although they are so large and are driven by strong winds, they are steered by a very small rudder wherever the pilot wants to go. [5]Likewise the tongue is a small part of the body, but it makes great boasts. Consider what a great forest is set on fire by a small spark. [6]The tongue also is a fire, a world of evil among the parts of the body. It corrupts the whole person, sets the whole course of his life on fire, and is itself set on fire by hell.
> [7]All kinds of animals, birds, reptiles and creatures of the sea are being tamed and have been tamed by man, [8]but no man can tame the tongue. It is a restless evil, full of deadly poison.

James compares the tongue to a bit, a rudder, a fire and a wild animal. He is a master of helpful analogies. With such vivid mental pictures, how can we miss the point? The tongue is powerful, and we need to pay close attention to how ours is used. Our lives will be used for good or for evil depending largely on how we learn to control this tiny part of the body.

James' practical teaching style reflects years of experience in the ministry (by this time 12-15 years), and his analogies are very relatable. For example, three of the four major crops grown in Judea were figs, olives and grapes! (The fourth was wheat.) If you are given to many words, learn from this seasoned speaker.

> [9]With the tongue we praise our Lord and Father, and with it we curse men, who have been made in God's likeness. [10]Out of the same mouth come praise and cursing. My brothers, this should not be. [11]Can both fresh water and salt water flow from the same spring? [12]My brothers, can a fig tree bear olives, or a grapevine bear figs? Neither can a salt spring produce fresh water.

The tongue can hurt deeply. Wielded carelessly, it is an instrument of Satan. Why does James dwell so long on the problem of the tongue? Because it was such a great need! Preach to the needs! This portion of the word of God is fully current today. It may have been first written down nineteen and a half centuries ago, but the heart and tongue of man (and woman) remains unchanged.

? How do you think that your tongue is being used? Have you been told you use it to hurt rather than to help and encourage? Is there far more positive coming from your mouth than negative? Name two people who would be the best ones to give you feedback on your speech and the ways you communicate.

> [13]Who is wise and understanding among you? Let him show it by his good life, by deeds done in the humility that comes from wisdom. [14]But if you harbor bitter envy and selfish ambition in your hearts, do not boast about it or deny the truth. [15]Such "wisdom" does not come down from heaven but is earthly, unspiritual, of the devil. [16]For where you have envy and selfish ambition, there you find disorder and every evil practice.
>
> [17]But the wisdom that comes from heaven is first of all pure; then peace-loving, considerate, submissive, full of mercy and good fruit, impartial and sincere. [18]Peacemakers who sow in peace raise a harvest of righteousness.

There are *two* sorts of wisdom: earthly (of the devil) and heavenly (godly). This section of James challenges the reader to the very core; it challenges every church to the very pith, because it lays bare the human heart. This is a crucial passage because at some point, even in the kingdom of God, you *will* be passed over, mistreated, ignored, or tempted to lash back. We live in an imperfect world, and if we have been hurt in our (small) earthly families, how much more likely are we to be hurt in our very large spiritual family?

It's easy to see how much the devil is behind conventional "wisdom" regarding pressure, getting ahead, feeling good about ourselves and many other topics. The world says, "Exalt yourself." God says, "Deny yourself"—*crucify it!* Are you wise? James gives us the traits of true wisdom. God's wisdom is:

- *pure*: not mixed with anything else (in particular not with demonic wisdom); purely motivated, pure in thought, word and deed.
- *peace-loving*: It does not retaliate, as the temptation must have been in troubled first-century Palestine. Though Christians must never become soft on sin or sentimental in regard to discipline, neither must we follow the way of violence.
- *considerate*: Do we *really* put others first? It begins with weighing our words, even before they are articulated!
- *submissive*: literally, "obedient, compliant." It isn't rebellious; it's open to persuasion. Are *you?*
- *full of mercy and good fruit*: God is looking for concrete changes, results.
- *impartial:* never taking the side of the unjust, never blinded by a bribe. Do we consistently act in our own self-interest, or do we *often* cede to others and trust God who rewards our acts of righteousness? The world needs spiritual leaders, men and women whose thinking and morality is not unquestioningly received from others, but carefully thought out in the brilliant light of the Scriptures.
- *sincere*: literally, "unhypocritical" (*anupokritos*).

Wisdom in the Bible isn't so much an *intellectual* quality as a *moral* quality. That's why the "wise" can turn out to be fools, and the "foolish" may be the wisest of all. Fundamentally, there are two and only two kinds of wisdom. Are you wise? Do you control your impulses and bridle your tongue?

Let's close this chapter with some well-known and much appreciated (conventional) wisdom:

> He who knows not and knows not that he knows not—
>   he is a fool, shun him!
> He who knows not and knows that he knows not—
>   he is simple, teach him!
> He who knows and knows not that he knows—
>   he is asleep, wake him!
> He who knows and knows that he knows—
>   he is wise, follow him!

?   Give some examples of things that are earthly and unspiritual, but nevertheless, may seem like "wisdom" to us. Which of the traits of true wisdom challenge you the most?

5

Macho Mist
JAMES 4

We have seen how the troubled political situation of first-century Palestine tempted many Christians to go to one of two extremes: condoning (or even benefiting from) the exploitation of the poor, or violent reaction against their aristocratic Jewish brothers or against the Romans. Chapter 4 of James continues in the "no-nonsense" style, written to call us to our spiritual senses.

> *¹What causes fights and quarrels among you? Don't they come from your desires that battle within you? ²You want something but don't get it. You kill and covet, but you cannot have what you want. You quarrel and fight. You do not have, because you do not ask God. ³When you ask, you do not receive, because you ask with wrong motives, that you may spend what you get on your pleasures.*

James is well aware of the tension within the Jewish Christian community. The people of God, instead of appealing to God in prayer, are trying to force his hand in order to receive material blessings. According to James, these outer tensions are only a reflection of the inner conflicts raging in the hearts of faithless and worldly Christians. Keep these facts in mind because they help us make sense of James' extremely strong words to the community.

Did they literally murder? Commentators have come up with many possible interpretations which soften the apparent thrust of the verse. Yet when we understand the politically perilous situation in Palestine—which led to a massive war with the Romans less than 20 years later and the ultimate destruction of Jerusalem Jesus had prophesied in Matthew 24—it seems probable that some Christians actually had become accomplices to murder. Or, if they hadn't been personally involved

in assassinations, had supported political factions with terror-
ist methods. During this time many wealthy Jews were mur-
dered as collaborators with the Romans and oppressors of
brother Israelites.

Here is a modern-day application question: Is it right for a
disciple to support ultra-radical organizations (which may even
support violence) such as the Neo-Nazis, National Front, Palestine Liberation Organization (PLO), Irish Republican Army
(IRA), or the Klu Klux Klan (KKK)? To ask the question is to
answer it! No, our first-century brothers were probably not
murdering anyone themselves, but they were influenced to
support or to condone political movements encouraging as-
sassination.

Our human tendency is to take things into our own hands.
The proper way to acquire what you want is to rely on God.
We say, "Pray as if everything depended on God and work as if
everything depends on you." There is a lot of truth in this
saying, but it can be taken too far. We must allow room for
God's wrath (Romans 12:19). This does not mean Christians
can't vote or become politically active, but the temptations to
worldliness—and the loss of our real purpose and our real values—are strong in the political arena, as many a fallen politi-
cian will verify.

James rebukes these worldly men for seeking pleasure before seeking God. When will the world learn the lesson that
happiness comes not when we get what we want, but when we
do what is right? Or, as Paul put it, "godliness with content-
ment is great gain" (1 Timothy 6:6).

So how about us? Are our prayers centered round what we
want, or do we sincerely pray, "*Thy* will be done"? "Spending
on our pleasures" means more than luxury items, desserts,
etc. "Our pleasures" means doing as *we* please, passing the cup
of suffering instead of drinking it to the dregs (Matthew 26:36-
46).

? Are there examples in your life of things you have not received because you have
tried to work them out yourself instead of asking God? What might be some examples in your life of asking God, but asking with the wrong motives? How do you
keep your motives purified?

⁴You adulterous people, don't you know that friendship with the world is hatred toward God? Anyone who chooses to be a friend of the world becomes an enemy of God.

Worldliness is tantamount to spiritual adultery! In the OT, Israel was often called "adulterous" for going after idols (Baal, Asherah, Molech, Chemosh, and others) or for making alliances with foreign nations instead of trusting in God. But spiritual adultery is a threat to the modern-day people of God, too. We are in the world, but must not be of the world (John 17:14-18).

Are we flirting with the world? Can you in good conscience answer the following questions in the negative?

- Am I tempted to miss church meetings in order to be with non-Christian friends?
- Do I work overtime without a thought, yet complain about extra church meetings?
- Do I happily save and spend for holidays, yet stingily give to world missions?
- Do I "cheat" on my contribution pledge?
- Do I pretend to be more devoted than I am? Am I more "committed" when others are around?
- Do others sometimes comment that my dress and demeanor are worldly?
- Do I take a second (lustful) look at attractive women or men?
- Do I take a second (lustful) look at things such as cars, clothes and other objects?
- Do I grow sleepy during sermons and other messages, or does my pulse quicken?
- Do I care more about non-Christians' opinions of me than about *God's* view of me?
- Is there anything in this world that has a stronger grip on my heart, mind, soul and strength than God, his word, his will and his movement?

? Which of the questions above challenge you the most? Who in your life knows well the struggle you have with these things?

Spiritual adultery: How easy it is to flirt with the world if we fail to guard our hearts (Proverbs 4:23). If there is any conspicuous area of weakness or sin, be careful! What may seem minor at first may in the end lead you down the slippery path. For a full exposition of how spiritual adultery works, read Proverbs 7 with these things in mind. Take this to heart: adultery is grounds for divorce. If we are being adulterous (worldly), God has every right to divorce us.

⁵Or do you think Scripture says without reason that the spirit he caused to live in us envies intensely? ⁶But he gives us more grace. That is why Scripture says:
"God opposes the proud
but gives grace to the humble."

"The Spirit he caused to live within us envies intensely," as one translation puts it (NIV), or "God yearns jealously for the spirit that he has made to dwell in us" (NRSV), because it is in the nature of God: He will tolerate no rivals for his love. Yes, God is a jealous God (Exodus 34:14), and to be "torn between two lovers" is not just to "feel like a fool," but to be one!

"God opposes the proud" (Proverbs 3:34) is one of the most often quoted OT verses in the NT. In the Bible, pride is not always a bad thing. In the OT it is often negative, as in "Pride goes before a fall" (Proverbs 16:18); but in the NT it is usually positive, as in "I take great pride in you" (2 Corinthians 7:4). It all depends what the pride is rooted in and what the underlying attitude is.

If you feel ineffective, frustrated, unproductive—in short, "opposed"—then it may well be (though not necessarily) that God is opposing you. Now any reasonable man or woman will agree that it's a poor choice to have God as your opponent. When the hand of the Lord is against us, he is only trying to get our attention (and affection) turned back to him.

? How deeply convinced are you that humility is an incredible quality that you want in your life? What do you do to demonstrate your conviction? When have you learned from experience the truth that God opposes the proud?

Warning: the following section is highly theological. May cause drowsiness. DO NOT attempt to read while pregnant or operating heavy machinery.

Excursus: OT Quotations in the NT

You may notice occasionally, when looking up an OT passage cited in the NT, that the quotation may be slightly different from the OT passage in your Bible. For instance, the quotation of Proverbs 3:34 in James 4:6 diverges slightly from the Hebrew OT. This is because NT writers usually cite the LXX, or *Septuagint*, the Greek translation of the OT Scriptures. This was a third-century B.C. translation from the original Hebrew/Aramaic into Greek, which was widely spoken at that time. It's called the LXX because, according to legend, it was translated by seventy scholars ("seventy" is *septuaginta*, in Latin). The original reads:

Im-lalletsim hu'-yalits wela'aniyyim yitten-chen—or, for those whose Hebrew may be rusty,

> *He mocks proud mockers,*
> > *but gives grace to the humble* (NIV).

> *Towards the scorners he is scornful,*
> > *but to the humble he shows favor* (NRSV).

The sense is the same as in the NT reference, though the nuance has changed. The LXX text reads: *kyrios hyperephanois antitassetai tapeinois de didosin charin*—which is exactly reproduced in the NT, except for the first phrase. (*kyrios* [the Lord] has become *theos* [God]—a minor difference, though it reflects the first Christians' confidence that Jesus is God, since "Lord" and "God" are more or less interchangeable in biblical thought.)

The LXX was the Bible of the majority of first-century disciples. They were more comfortable with Greek than Hebrew; even Latin would not eclipse Greek as the language of choice in the Roman world for another century or two.

Issues of language and translation cannot be ignored. As we have seen, with careful analysis this sort of surface "contradiction" between NT citations and OT verses vanishes; there has been an intermediate translation. Finally, occasionally discrepancies occur simply because the writer is quoting rather freely, just as preachers today may paraphrase a passage instead of quoting it strictly.

So we see that the NT writers were not twisting words; they were being faithful to their Bible. Moreover, God's inspiration involves this special translation situation! While the LXX is not an inspired translation of the OT, the inspired writers of the NT, faithful to the inherent sense of the passages they deal with, convey exactly what God wanted them write.

End of excursus. It is now safe to resume speed.

> [7]*Submit yourselves, then, to God. Resist the devil, and he will flee from you.* [8]*Come near to God and he will come near to you. Wash your hands, you sinners, and purify your hearts, you double-minded.* [9]*Grieve, mourn and wail. Change your laughter to mourning and your joy to gloom.* [10]*Humble yourselves before the Lord, and he will lift you up.*

Submitting to God (not taking the law into your own hands) is the way of peace described in chapter 3. We must resist the devil; he is the real enemy! And, as you have no doubt heard, the devil is a coward, and he will flee. But expect him at an "opportune time"—inopportune for you, opportune for him (Luke 4:13)!

Verses 7-10 sound like some of the denunciations of the OT prophets: impassioned, hard-line, radical and insisting on righteousness. Sometimes even the people of God need a "wake-up call." Let's not be double-minded (tempted to serve God *and* self, the kingdom *and* the world, which is spiritual adultery). Let's serve one Lord and one Lord only!

> [11]*Brothers, do not slander one another. Anyone who speaks against his brother or judges him speaks against the law and judges it. When you judge the law, you are not keeping it, but sitting in judgment on it.* [12]*There is only one Lawgiver and Judge, the one who is able to save and destroy. But you—who are you to judge your neighbor?*

To slander a fellow Jew was to disagree with what God said about love for neighbor. To slander is to speak against the Law, because the Law strictly forbade slander and defamation in Leviticus 19:16-17. (See also Psalm 15:3.) Slander is one of the *verboten* varieties of judging referred to earlier (see page 28),

> [13]*Now listen, you who say, "Today or tomorrow we will go to this or that city, spend a year there, carry on business and*

make money." ¹⁴Why, you do not even know what will happen tomorrow. What is your life? You are a mist that appears for a little while and then vanishes. ¹⁵Instead, you ought to say, "If it is the Lord's will, we will live and do this or that." ¹⁶As it is, you boast and brag. All such boasting is evil.

This passage, very helpful in studying sin with those who want to become disciples, is actually directed at the growing *merchant class* who are making their plans without putting God into the picture. Their main aim is money. These were not the aristocracy, but those who profited economically at the expense of their fellow Jews. Love of God and neighbor were taking a back seat.

Planning is good, and many verses remind us of the importance of counsel and planning. Everyone is very interested in his or her own future; that's where the temptation to pride comes in. Dream, plan, dare—yes! But before we make plans, it would be good to remember that we are nothing but a mist. Mist, fog, vapor and smoke don't boast. They are not around long enough to brag, so they remain humble. "Macho mist"? That does not compute!

Leaving God out of your calculations? Put him back in, and thank him that you are in his calculations! (Read Amos 6:1-7, and be convicted!)

¹⁷Anyone, then, who knows the good he ought to do and doesn't do it, sins.

Finally, the sin James denounces in 4:13-16 falls into the category of sins of "omission," as opposed to sins of "commission." Sins of omission entail neglect. Do we regularly rationalize *doing* our will and *not doing* the will of God—almost subconsciously—losing our focus on his will and drifting mentally?

Actually, God expects us to internalize his word, so that we don't need a list of rules to tell us what is right (Psalm 40:8). Living by principle is spiritual maturity. The principles of the Bible become so deeply ingrained that his word becomes second nature, like riding a bicycle, cooking and other things you never, ever forget how to do.

Macho mist? No way! We need the Lord in the picture. To rely on him, to pray to him. You see, in the words of a popular song, "You got to pray (pray), pray (pray), you got to pray just to make it today!" Which brings us to chapter 6.

? When there has been sin in your life, have you had the attitude described in 4: 9-10? Are you in any way fearful of such an attitude? Why does it always lead to a good result? What plans are you making right now for your life? Have you completely surrendered and submitted those to God?

6

You've Got to Pray
JAMES 5

Times may be hard. Life is not fair. All things are not equal. (I don't know who ever said they were!) Temptations, trials and tests squeeze us every day of every year of our life. And even then, life is short. "Mists" are very needy, and the shortness of life helps us to see our need for our Creator. When "trouble's in our way," what do we do? Are we greeting it with grace, facing it with faith? In first-century Israel, as now in many parts of the world, many get caught up in completely unfair circumstances. If this world is all there is, what tragedy! But if there is a God in heaven, everything is different.

> *¹Now listen, you rich people, weep and wail because of the misery that is coming upon you. ²Your wealth has rotted, and moths have eaten your clothes. ³Your gold and silver are corroded. Their corrosion will testify against you and eat your flesh like fire. You have hoarded wealth in the last days. ⁴Look! The wages you failed to pay the workmen who mowed your fields are crying out against you. The cries of the harvesters have reached the ears of the Lord Almighty. ⁵You have lived on earth in luxury and self-indulgence. You have fattened yourselves in the day of slaughter. ⁶You have condemned and murdered innocent men, who were not opposing you.*

Who are these people James is verbally attacking? They are the landed aristocracy—whether non-Christian Jews or disciples who supported the exploiters of the poor—and they received a red-hot rebuke from the lips of the Lord. These affluent, well-dressed, extravagant and overweight people even took the poor to court, exploiting their position to squeeze every last penny from their less fortunate neighbors.

Withholding of wages, even overnight, was roundly condemned in the word of God, as was cheating a laborer by underpaying him: Deuteronomy 24:14-15; Leviticus 19:13;

Jeremiah 22:13; and Malachi 3:5 show God's fiery indignation against this sort of immorality.

Concerning "the day of slaughter" (5:5), after the slaughter of an animal, as much meat was consumed as possible, since without refrigeration, "leftovers" were useful only if they were dried and then salted. In fact meat was a rare luxury for the poor, except during festivals and times of sacrifice. The "fat cats" being condemned in the above verses were committing the sin of the sons of Eli. (See 1 Samuel 2:12-17.)

Sidenote: if the Israelites had been faithful to God and presented their animal sacrifices while showing genuine concern for their neighbors, there would have been enough meat for all. And considering all the sin of the people of God under the old covenant, that would have meant a lot of sacrificing, a lot of meat. So, the rich would have been leading the way! Deuteronomy 15:7-12 shows the kind of openhanded sharing the people of God should be known for. As is always the case, we see the perfection of God's perfect system. Don't blame God for the sin that spoils everything; it is *man* who has sabotaged the plan of God.

They were "condemning and murdering" (5:6) innocent men: the poor. Either they (actively) cast their vote against the lower castes, or (passively) failed to defend them. Isaiah 58 and many other passages show the heart of God and the duty of man in this regard.

(Incidentally, James' denunciation was not sinful. His rebuke of the rich did not qualify as slander. No, "love of neighbor" does not mean it's wrong to speak out against injustice, but violence and hostile speech are forbidden.)

? Are you a passionate advocate for the poor? What deeds are in your life that show you have the same heart for the poor as God does? In what ways do you need to see yourself as among the "wealthy"?

> *⁷Be patient, then, brothers, until the Lord's coming. See how the farmer waits for the land to yield its valuable crop and how patient he is for the autumn and spring rains. ⁸You too, be patient and stand firm, because the Lord's coming is near. ⁹Don't grumble against each other, brothers, or you will be judged. The Judge is standing at the door!*
>
> *¹⁰Brothers, as an example of patience in the face of suffering, take the prophets who spoke in the name of the Lord. ¹¹As*

*you know, we consider blessed those who have persevered.
You have heard of Job's perseverance and have seen what the
Lord finally brought about. The Lord is full of compassion
and mercy.*

Patience is the order of the day, not *grumbling*. God will take care of the oppressors; there is no need to fear. "The Lord's coming" almost certainly refers to his judgment on the rich, as is so often the case in the OT. James offers two examples of patience in the face of suffering to help the Palestinian Christians through this testing time:

- *The prophets*: They suffered because they were opposed by the religious establishment. Yet they preached on and so should we!
- *Job*: He maintained his integrity despite not understanding why he was suffering. (That's hard!) He never was filled in on the big picture! Whether or not all of our questions are answered, we must remain steadfast.

*[12]Above all, my brothers, do not swear—not by heaven or
by earth or by anything else. Let your "Yes" be yes, and your
"No," no, or you will be condemned.*

What exactly James means by "do not swear" is open to interpretation. Perhaps he is referring to the type of oath taken by those who would gladly have done away with Paul in Acts 23:12. This is possible, and would nicely explain the jump to the injunction against swearing, but leaves us wondering whether this is really what James had in mind.

"Swearing by heaven or earth" reminds us of the various species of oath distinguished by the Pharisees (see Matthew 23). But how would this fit the context? We should look for continuity of thought whenever possible, giving the writer the benefit of the doubt that he was a clear thinker and orderly communicator.

Certainly we find here echoes of Matthew 5:33-37; apparently the Jewish people were very fond of oath-taking. Maybe it's the temptation to dishonesty that comes when times are hard. In times of emergency, the means seem to justify the ends: expedience takes precedence over ethics; overconfidence overshadows objectivity. So perhaps James is referring to any sort of rash oath (see Ecclesiastes 5:4-7) that might be taken by someone under great strain.

Some scholars have suggested James' point is that when we feel the stress and impatience of trials, rather than swear (5:12) we should pray (5:13). This fits nicely into the section that follows.

Whatever James had in mind, we can all certainly agree there should be no need for a true disciple to take an oath, since we must be men and women of our word. Is your "Yes" really yes, and your "No," no? Can you be counted on? Are you a person of integrity? It shows in big things and in little things:

- Do you forget commitments you've made? Promise things lightly?
- Are you honest, or do you shade the truth?
- Would you lie for your boss? Would you say, "He's not in" when he's sitting right next to you?
- Do you often arrive late to church meetings? (Have to sit in the back?)
- Would you get high commendation and good references from your employer?
- Do people say you are an excuse-maker? Or are you one who takes responsibility?
- Do you exaggerate? Do you flatter?
- Are you a good tenant? Is your landlord/landlady happy with you?
- Do you pay your bills on time? Has your phone ever been cut off? Do you owe back taxes?
- Are you in good control of your bank account(s)?
- When you say you'll return a call (as in an answering machine message), do you?
- Are you automotively trustworthy? Receive speeding tickets? Parking fines?
- Financially, do you give first to the Lord and then take care of your own needs?
- When you set a goal, do you work at it until you've succeeded?
- Are you trusted with responsibility, or passed over for someone more trustworthy?

- Do you say "Amen" lightly, careless as to what it will take for you to change?
- Does your spiritual outside match your spiritual inside? Or are you the "hype type"? Do you feel like you are leading a double life?

? What questions in the list above challenge you the most? What do these things reveal about your character? How can God and your fellow disciples help you to change?

[13]Is any one of you in trouble? He should pray. Is anyone happy? Let him sing songs of praise. [14]Is any one of you sick? He should call the elders of the church to pray over him and anoint him with oil in the name of the Lord. [15]And the prayer offered in faith will make the sick person well; the Lord will raise him up. If he has sinned, he will be forgiven. [16]Therefore confess your sins to each other and pray for each other so that you may be healed. The prayer of a righteous man is powerful and effective.

James asks if any of us is "in trouble," harkening back to the "trials" (1:2). Troubles are part of the Christian life because troubles are part of life. Christianity promises no escape from hardship but rather, offers the strength to overcome. So if you have troubles, how much are you praying? It is so much easier to react in a worldly way, isn't it? The proper response to trouble is prayer (not resentment, complaining or retaliation), just as songs of praise are the proper response to God's good gifts (1:17). God cares, and he assures us he will stand by us. When he is working powerfully among us we can "sing and be happy." (See Proverbs 29:6, and check your heart.)

What about the "prayer of faith" for a sick disciple? James says we should call for the elders of the church and anoint the sick person with oil. First, the assumption is that there are elders in the church. In most societies in James' day, and in many societies even today, elders in the community (those whom the town look to for guidance and arbitration) naturally became the elders of the church. In fragmented twentieth-century Western society, where "community" has become an elusive and optional concept, church elders will not necessarily pull the same weight in the community they would have in the first century. Anyway, James told them to call for the elders because they were the most spiritual people in the church; their prayer was most likely to be effective (5:16).

The anointing with oil may be (a) medicinal, (b) an expression of faith, or (c) a preparation allowing God's Spirit to work. This isn't the usual word for anoint (*chrio,* whence *Christos*), but rather the word (*aleipho*), meaning "to oil, to smear, rub with oil." When a king was anointed, *chrio* was the word used; when someone was sick, *aleipho* was the word.

Most NT interpreters believe the anointing in James was medicinal (option "a"), since olive oil was commonly used to maintain health or cleanse wounds. Applying oil was a part of one's personal hygiene, which is why Jesus says if there is oil on your head no one will suspect you are fasting (Matthew 6:17). *Not* putting oil on your head would be the giveaway. Suffice it to say that it's okay for Christians to look their best!

If the anointing is an expression of faith (option "b"), James is saying, in effect, "Get up! Put on your oil, prepare for a return to the mainstream of life. You're going to be healed!"

If option "c" is right, we are left a bit mystified as to why the anointing is necessary and why the usual word for (religious) anointing *(chrio)* is not used. This possibility therefore seems unlikely.

Make your own decision. Whatever you believe, it seems the practice of anointing was probably cultural, not bound on all Christians of all ages. So pray for healing, pray in faith, get spiritual men and women to pray for you, and expect a recovery. As for the oil, among disciples that is a matter of opinion.

Notice the connection between health and forgiveness of sins. Many biblical passages relate *spiritual* health to *physical* health, especially in Psalms and Proverbs. Even 1 Corinthians 11 discusses this in relation to the communion. It is heartening to see that modern medicine is increasingly acknowledging this connection.

As disciples, we confess our sins to other disciples, not to a holy man behind a curtain. That's because in real Christianity there is an openness, a vulnerability and sense of family not found in the religious world. Do you confess only to one individual to the exclusion of all others? Do you have several strong Christian friends, or only one? We all need many deep relationships to remain faithful to God for a lifetime. When we are open about our sin with several people, they can each pray powerfully and effectively for us. Elijah was like us, and his prayers stopped the rain for over three years. Certainly praying for one another works, but this is unrealistic and ineffective when there is lack of honesty and openness.

About Openness

Merely confessing sins to one another obviously can become an excuse for not changing. Proverbs 28:13 says, "No one who conceals transgressions will prosper, but one who confesses and renounces them will obtain mercy" (NRSV). God is not just interested in confession. Often disciples spend a lot of time chatting about sin without really changing. One wonders if all this does not become quite tedious to our God. What about *repentance?* Two questions we must put to ourselves:
• Do I confess my sin?
• Do I change, or am I ever confessing the same sin?

But there is another area of openness current in Christian circles. Its the pseudo-openness of confessing "bad attitudes." In an appeal to Matthew 18:15-17 a brother or sister may say, "I just need to confess my bad attitudes against you. After all, Jesus said we should go to our brother."

Well, to begin with, Matthew 18 does not deal with confessing bad feelings. This passage concerns a brother who has sinned against you, not a brother against whom you are harboring sinful thoughts. If someone has, in fact, sinned against you, the second stage is getting others involved. Stage three brings the case before the assembly *(ekklesia,* "church, or part of the church") for group assistance. Ask your friend, "Are you willing to bring this before the church if necessary?" Nine times out of ten their answer will be no.

A lot of abuse is dished out; a lot of ventilation of bitterness, or "emotional vomiting" goes on in the name of Matthew 18. The mature disciple will train himself to take captive every thought to make it obedient to Christ (2 Corinthians 10:5). There is little, if any, need to confess every weird thought that runs through our heads. Rather than talking about these little attitudes (which may feed them), in most cases we should just crucify them!

Yes, openness and honesty are important, and it can be dangerous to stuff feelings, but Matthew 18 is not a passage providing biblical warrant to belch out negative feelings in the name of openness!

To sum up, if you have sinned against someone in word, thought or deed, you are not necessarily obligated to go to the person and confess the mess. Likewise, next time a brother or sister confesses to you negative feelings towards another disciple, do take it seriously but *don't* feel compelled to direct him to the person he or she has ill will towards. If we all talked with each other every time our feelings were hurt in some way, we (not to mention the assembly) would be endlessly tied up in discussing feelings and attitudes, and thus wasting precious time God has given us for better things. Thus, we need to develop both sensitivity and emotional toughness.

> [17]*Elijah was a man just like us. He prayed earnestly that it would not rain, and it did not rain on the land for three and a half years.* [18]*Again he prayed, and the heavens gave rain, and the earth produced its crops.*

The point is that prayer works. The reference here is to 1 Kings 17-18, where Elijah, through the strength of his relationship with God, changes history (and meteorology). Prayer is a central part of both spiritual and physical health.

> [9]*My brothers, if one of you should wander from the truth and someone should bring him back,* [20]*remember this: Whoever turns a sinner from the error of his way will save him from death and cover over a multitude of sins.*

If sin has progressed quite far, beyond the point of mere sickness, so that a brother or sister has actually wandered from the truth, there is still hope—but only if another disciple cares enough to get personally involved. Apparently some of the Christians in the communities James was addressing had been overcome by the trials (1:2). They hadn't persevered; they'd given in to worldly ways. We all stumble (3:2), but not all wander, and those who do are either brought back or become casualties of war.

The "multitude of sins" being covered through someone's restoration back into the kingdom of God (5:20) is obviously that of the person being restored, not an accumulation of merit on the part of the disciple doing the restoring. May God help us bring back into the fold *every* wandering sheep. The "twelve tribes" may be scattered among the nations, but there's no need for them to be lost there! Indeed, we are *in* the world but not *of* the world.

Conclusion

The letter of James is especially practical in societies where economic inequality and political tensions run high. Around the world at any given time there are over a hundred wars and civil wars in progress. This being the case, James has a special relevance—unlike any other NT letter—for disciples in societies that are consuming themselves in envy, slander, murder and strife of all kinds. God has made his word cover all possible situations, which is another evidence that his word is true and that behind his word is One who loves us and cares for our well-being.

This being the case, let us pray. Only then will be have the stamina required to, one day, attain that coveted crown of life.

? Who do you know who has a great prayer life characterized by faith? What can you learn from this person? Do you believe that you, too, can pray like this? Write down the names of three people you know who have "wandered from the truth." What can you do for each of them to bring them back?

Part II

THE LOVE OF LIFE

1 AND 2 PETER

"Whoever would love life
and see good days
must keep his tongue from evil
and his lips from deceitful speech.
He must turn from evil and do good;
he must seek peace and pursue it."

1 PETER 3:10-11

We all want to see *good* days—a rich and meaningful life. The Rock himself tells us the secret in his powerful, yet humble, memoirs. Come and learn from Jesus' chosen leader, Simon bar Jonah.

7

Peter: A Rock's Memoirs
INTRODUCTION

Peter was called "The Rock" (John 1:42; Matthew 16:18) for the strength of his character and leadership—whether present or future, and because of his prominent role in the early church. Although he was chief apostle (at least until the time of Paul), in Jesus' inner circle, spokesman for the company of believers, miracle-worker, elder and much, much more, Peter never allowed prominence to go to his head. He never bullied others, and kept the common touch in his leadership style. We read in 1 Peter 5, in the 1993 paraphrase-translation *The Message*:

> *I know what it's like to be a leader, in on Christ's sufferings as well as the coming glory. Here's my concern: that you care for God's flock with all the diligence of a shepherd. Not because you have to, but because you want to please God. Not calculating what you can get out of it, but acting spontaneously. Not bossily telling others what to do, but tenderly showing them the way... But all of you, leaders and followers alike, are to be down to earth with each other, for "God has had it with the proud, but takes delight in just plain people."*

This captures the spirit and the secret of Peter's influence. He left behind for us 1 and 2 Peter, his "memoirs," a Rock's memoirs.

Apostleship

Peter was an apostle, one of the original Twelve and a witness of Christ's resurrection. The apostles stood ready to be dispatched *wherever, whenever.* They were servants, they were evangelistic, and they had great dreams to start new churches the world over.

Audience

In 1 Peter, the Rock wrote to five regions of western Asia Minor (modern Turkey). Nero persecuted Christians in Rome, yet it seems that provincial governors took the law into their own hands and did some persecuting of their own. In all likelihood the disciples of Asia Minor had heard of the hardships endured by the European Christians.

History would repeat itself some thirty years later under the cruel Domitian. Nero reigned 54-68 A.D.; his persecution of the Christians started in 64, the year 1 Peter was written. Domitian ruled in Rome from 81-96 A.D.; it was in the end of his reign that he sponsored a more severe persecution. God prepared the saints for this severe time of testing through the revelation given to John years in advance and recorded in the book of Revelation.

In his second letter, written shortly before his death (upside-down crucifixion according to tradition, almost certainly some form of crucifixion according to John 21:18-19), Peter warns the church against the legion of false teachers who were already beginning to overrun the Christian church. Each letter is powerful and to the point, in the style of Peter himself.

Personal

If the life of Peter were going to be made into a movie, it could be called *From Rolling Stone to Rocky.* Before the Lord called him, his character was more rash than rational. His impetuousness is proverbial, and he was given to bad habits, for instance, swearing (Matthew 26:74; 1 Peter 4:3). Simon Peter lacked mission in his life (Luke 5:10). As a fisherman he was used to discouragement—long, unproductive nights of fishing—and must have been developing the patience that would serve him well in the future in his capacity as a major church leader. At the same time he spoke his mind plainly (Matthew 16:22), was quick to respond (Galatians 2:11; 2 Peter 3:14-15), and was always ready to learn from his mistakes and move on (Luke 22:23; see Jeremiah 8:4). All these are qualities which endear him to every generation of disciples. It is easy to believe that Peter loved life, as he talked about in 1 Peter 3.

Peter was totally transformed by the Lord. He became bold and confident (Acts 4:12-13). His responsibility level shows a steady increase throughout life—a great model for the growing disciple:

- follower of Jesus (Mark 1:18)
- apostle (Mark 3:14)
- chief apostle (Matthew 16:18)
- leader of Jerusalem church (Acts 2:14)
- traveling missions evangelist (Acts 8:14, 9:32)
- martyr (John 21:19)

Are you growing like that, always taking it higher in your walk with God? Peter was committed unto death (John 21:18; the non-canonical 1 Clement 5:4), and left us two letters (1 and 2 Peter) and a gospel (Mark, which was written through Peter's influence, according to second-century church history). Let's take a brief glance at the two letters Peter wrote.

1 Peter

This letter was written by the aged apostle to disciples in Western Turkey (Asia Minor) from Rome (Compare 1 Peter 5:13 with Revelation, where "Babylon" stands for Rome) in a climate of opposition. After apparently starting the Fire of Rome, 64 A.D., Nero Caesar implicated the Christians who became scapegoats. Many in Rome were arrested, tortured and executed in a grisly manner. While the disciples in Asia Minor may not have suffered in exactly this way, the official stance of Rome surely would have made life more difficult for Christians anywhere in the empire.

Christians were soon to lose their enjoyment of imperial protection under the umbrella of Judaism, after the Roman destruction of Jerusalem in 70 A.D. Peter deeply desired that the disciples stand up gracefully and graciously under the pressures they were facing, just as Christ Jesus himself faced opposition from the world.

Following is a thumbnail sketch of the letter:

Chapter 1: *Salvation* is awesome. It's worth it, yet it is constantly being tested, especially now in this time of persecution. Let's get focused!

Chapter 2: *Suffering* is an integral part of following Jesus. Sacrifices are part of our priesthood. Persecution is to be expected.

Chapter 3: *Strain* is a result of such conditions. Hardships test relationships. Strive for familial, congregational and social harmony. Noah, too, stood his ground amidst opposition.

Chapter 4: *Stamina* and strength are everything. Arm yourselves with the attitude of endurance. If you don't drown in the (real) flood of sin, then you will survive this life's judgment.

Chapter 5: *Submission* to the leaders and the hand of God is crucial. Trust God; beware of the devil. Finally, suffering is normal, yet (good news!) it's only temporary.

2 Peter

This letter was written to protect the church from false prophets. A fuller introduction to the historical situation, as well as an overview of church history, will be provided in Chapter 14. Here is a working outline:

Chapter 1: *Grace* and *growth* come only through the knowledge of God.

Chapter 2: *Twisted gospels* and *twisted lives* characterize the false teachers.

Chapter 3: *Fear God* and *further your knowledge* of him, and you will never fall away.

Truly the memoirs of the Rock are every bit as bold, blunt and moving as the apostle himself. Get ready to be blessed by your study of these great epistles!

? In what ways do you identify with Peter? How does his life give you great hope for yours? How does his life give you great hope for others that you know? Look carefully at the words used to summarize the message of each of the chapters of 1 Peter. Which of these words hits a nerve in your life and why?

8

Invisible but Invincible
1 PETER 1

How can reasonable men and women in this day and age honestly believe in a God they cannot see, a Savior they have never met, and a spiritual world seemingly wholly beyond the investigation of science? Peter and the other eyewitnesses of Jesus had an unfair advantage, did they not? Yet Christians the world over *do* believe without seeing and enjoy their relationship with God, just as our first-century brothers and sisters did. In fact, faith *is* a kind of seeing. After seeing the truth of the Bible and the love of God, it could fairly be asked, "How can reasonable men and women honestly *not* believe in God and in his Son, Jesus Christ?"

In this same assurance of faith, Peter wrote his first letter to the scattered saints of Asia Minor. The time: the early 60s (A.D., of course!). Nero is on the throne. Persecution is mounting. The disciples need some real encouragement.

> *[1]Peter, an apostle of Jesus Christ,*
> *To God's elect, strangers in the world, scattered throughout Pontus, Galatia, Cappadocia, Asia and Bithynia, [2]who have been chosen according to the foreknowledge of God the Father, through the sanctifying work of the Spirit, for obedience to Jesus Christ and sprinkling by his blood:*
> *Grace and peace be yours in abundance.*

Peter is addressing God's elect. It should give us great security to know that God has chosen us! Whereas in the world election and corruption seem to go hand in hand, in the kingdom of God, election goes with commitment. That's rare both in political and religious circles. Living as disciples, going against the flow, swimming upstream, being willing to stand up and be counted can at times be uncomfortable. It feels strange.

So they are "strangers in the world" (1:1). Peter is comparing the feelings of estrangement and alienation the disciples had to the experience of God's people in OT times in foreign captivity. (Through Assyria, Babylon, Persia, etc., God disciplined his people as he vowed he would in Deuteronomy 28. Captivity stretched more or less from the eighth to the sixth centuries B.C.) How does it feel to be a stranger, an outsider, an alien, a non-citizen, an exile and a nomad, spiritually speaking? This world is not our home!

If God foreknows (knows in advance), isn't it a bit unfair that so many are born with no hope? First, God knows in advance like we may know the ending of a novel in advance, by jumping to the final chapter. But knowing the outcome in no way means you are responsible for it. Each character decides and acts in accordance with his own free will. God knows the end before the beginning because he is unbound by space and time. God is just, and no one will be punished or rewarded more than is deserved.

Men and women who earnestly seek God are chosen by him on account of their willingness to come to him. God's election *never* overrides our free will. In John 6:44-45 we see that (1) it is impossible to come to God unless he draws you, and (2) God won't draw you unless you listen to Jesus Christ. It's cooperative. You could say that God chooses those who choose him.

God calls us through the proclamation of the gospel. (Thus, it is impossible to hear the call without hearing and understanding the gospel.) A very handy passage on this is 2 Thessalonians 2:13-14. Calvinist theology (God has predestined you to eternal damnation or salvation) misunderstands the Scriptures, discourages evangelism, cheapens the Cross; it is widespread.[1]

"Sanctified and sprinkled": The Spirit sanctifies or makes us holy, committed, obedient disciples. We have also been sprinkled by his blood. In the OT, blood takes away sins (see Hebrews 9:22). That means we are saved. When we have *been* saved and *continue* to live as disciples, we will truly have grace

---

[1] For a detailed discussion of this see the chapter on Calvinism in *Prepared to Answer* by Gordon Ferguson, (Woburn, Mass: Discipleship Publications International, 1995) pp. 86-104.

and peace in abundance. Few people on earth enjoy this blessing because few are prepared to meet the cost in commitment.

³Praise be to the God and Father of our Lord Jesus Christ!
In his great mercy he has given us new birth into a living hope
through the resurrection of Jesus Christ from the dead, ⁴and
into an inheritance that can never perish, spoil or fade—kept
in heaven for you, ⁵who through faith are shielded by God's
power until the coming of the salvation that is ready to be
revealed in the last time.

"Praise be"...or, "Get fired-up!" In the original Greek, verses 3-9 form one long sentence! Peter is really bubbling over. The point: It's okay to enjoy your salvation. We love and appreciate much because we have been forgiven much (Luke 7:36-50).

We have been given new birth into a living hope. "Hope" in the Bible means more than a vague wish or a pathetic yearning. It means serious expectation. Hope usually has reference to the resurrection and the life of the world to come. Hope keeps us sweet instead of sour, positive instead of negative. This is essential because the world desperately needs and looks for hope. "Life to the full" for the average human being is only a fabrication of Hollywood, or the slim chance of winning the lottery. Even then, in our hearts we all know nothing will really change through luck alone.

"Inheritance": How would you like to receive a billionaire's inheritance? We have something far more valuable, untouched by mildew, sunlight, age, moth, theft, tax man or inflation. God has written his will, and we are the heirs (Galatians 4:7). We are in his will if we are doing his will (Matthew 7:21)!

Also, we are 100% shielded by God's power. What confidence the Christian should have! Nothing can destroy him or his salvation; God will allow no temptation to drag him away (1 Corinthians 10:13). Stay behind that shield; keep your faith strong! And you can be sure that anything God allows to come through that shield is something you can handle with his help. Otherwise, he would stop it cold.

⁶In this you greatly rejoice, though now for a little while you
may have had to suffer grief in all kinds of trials. ⁷These have

come so that your faith—of greater worth than gold, which perishes even though refined by fire—may be proved genuine and may result in praise, glory and honor when Jesus Christ is revealed. [8]Though you have not seen him, you love him; and even though you do not see him now, you believe in him and are filled with an inexpressible and glorious joy, [9]for you are receiving the goal of your faith, the salvation of your souls.

The "trials" would surely come, but, in this case, they would last only a while. The grief brought by the trials was eclipsed by the inexpressible and glorious joy (1:8) that comes when we appreciate our salvation.

"Praise, glory and honor": Both Peter and Paul (Romans 2:7) knew what it is all about. Don't you want to be praised by God? Some of us are too spiritual to desire what Peter and Paul desired—to hear "Well done, good and faithful servant!" In false humility we say, "I don't really want to be rewarded." But of course you do! Children often understand spiritual principles implicitly. Kids love to be praised. God is our Father, and how awesome we will feel about ourselves and our relationship with him when he says those encouraging words to us. Yes, we need his affection and his approval. We *thrive* on it. (For more on this, see C.S. Lewis' *The Weight of Glory and Other Essays.)*

"You have not seen him" (1:8). God *is* invisible, which is exactly why we live by faith, not by sight (2 Corinthians 5:7). Yet Peter's point is that invisible or not, with God on our side, in whatever trials we may be going through, we are invincible.

"The goal of your faith" (1:9). How should we answer the question "Isn't it selfish to focus on going to heaven?" By exclaiming, "Absolutely not!" Quite simply, salvation *is* the goal of our faith: Don't be embarrassed about this! Yet we should not think that people driven by impure motives will make it very far in the kingdom of God. Similar to marriage, it may be entered into from wrong or mixed motives, but the motivation will have to change or the relationship will not last. So it is not selfish to desire salvation

In fact, far from attempting to escape the pressures and responsibilities of the real world by looking forward to heaven, we embrace the pressures and triumph, shoulder the responsibilities and make this world a far better place, "soul by soul and silently."

People who love truth and commitment naturally want salvation (to be with their Lord). But those who prefer pleasure and excuses have no taste for spiritual things. So don't worry, whatever selfishness we may have in wanting to go to heaven will be burned away in the fires of testing.

? Write down a challenge you are facing right now. In what ways can God shield you and protect you? Can he still do it even if you cannot figure out how he will do it? Who do you know who is a good example of the kind of faith Peter describes?

> [10]*Concerning this salvation, the prophets, who spoke of the grace that was to come to you, searched intently and with the greatest care,* [11]*trying to find out the time and circumstances to which the Spirit of Christ in them was pointing when he predicted the sufferings of Christ and the glories that would follow.* [12]*It was revealed to them that they were not serving themselves but you, when they spoke of the things that have now been told you by those who have preached the gospel to you by the Holy Spirit sent from heaven. Even angels long to look into these things.*

"The prophets" (1:10): In this instance, the prophets are the Old Testament prophets. (In Ephesians 4:11, 3:5 and 2:20 the prophets are NT prophets. The context determines whether "prophets" means NT or OT variety.) The most understandable messianic prophecies for the beginning reader of the Bible are probably those in Isaiah, Zechariah, Psalms and a few other OT books.

"The angels" (1:12), out of the loop, are obsessively curious to see what's going on, to grasp God's incredible plan. The verb "to look into," *parakupsai* has the root meaning "to bend over, to see, steal a glance." (See Luke 24:12.)

> [13]*Therefore, prepare your minds for action; be self-controlled; set your hope fully on the grace to be given you when Jesus Christ is revealed.* [14]*As obedient children, do not conform to the evil desires you had when you lived in ignorance.* [15]*But just as he who called you is holy, so be holy in all you do;* [16]*for it is written: "Be holy, because I am holy."*
> [17]*Since you call on a Father who judges each man's work impartially, live your lives as strangers here in reverent fear.*

Since God's plan and kingdom are so awesome, get ready for action. Christianity takes discipline. Those who lack it learn it or die; there are no exceptions, as Proverbs teaches us (Proverbs 5:22-23). Lack of discipline is a killer; the undisciplined will ultimately bite the dust.

? What were the "evil desires you had when you lived in ignorance"? Are you living a holy life? For a challenge, read William Law's *Serious Call to a Devout and Holy Life.*

Fear? Is it really proper for a child to fear his father? Of course! But healthy respect for authority is in short supply these days. Are we really saved, or not? Should we live in continuous fear of being "zapped" by God for the merest trace of lukewarmness? No, all the saints are saved; yet there are degrees of reward in heaven. The reward at the disciple's judgment is not salvation; it's treasure in heaven (Matthew 6:20). The more you put into life in the kingdom, the more you get out of heaven. Doesn't it make sense that those who tried hardest will appreciate heaven the most? As the Lord said, "Where your treasure is, there your heart will be also" (Matthew 6:21).

> [18]For you know that it was not with perishable things such as silver or gold that you were redeemed from the empty way of life handed down to you from your forefathers, [19]but with the precious blood of Christ, a lamb without blemish or defect. [20]He was chosen before the creation of the world, but was revealed in these last times for your sake. [21]Through him you believe in God, who raised him from the dead and glorified him, and so your faith and hope are in God.

"The empty way of life" (1:18): Psychologist Carl Jung said many decades ago, "Emptiness is the central neurosis of our time." And he is right. We have all felt it, and any honest person will admit the emptiness of his life, the hole in his heart, the vacuum in his soul. Jesus Christ reverses the horror of a meaningless existence.

The Lamb (1:19), willing to be slaughtered, is our Savior who calls us to follow in his steps. God had it all planned. Sin didn't catch God off guard. He knew before he made Adam what mankind would need, and he held back nothing.

The Lamb was without blemish because he never sinned (Hebrews 2:18, 4:15). Imagine the pressure of knowing that if you blew it just once, it was all over. Jesus was the paragon of power, love and self-discipline. He is the Lamb of God who takes away the sins of the world, of every nation of the world (John 1:29). And does he ever! Salvation is full and free. Ultimately, existence is futile apart from Christ.

And through this same Lamb (1:21) we believe in God. Apart from Christ it is not fully possible to believe in God, because our picture of God will be distorted. Even sincere people in other religions cannot believe in the true God as a Bible-reader and -follower can; their religion, sadly, is some form or other of idolatry.

> ²²*Now that you have purified yourselves by obeying the truth so that you have sincere love for your brothers, love one another deeply, from the heart.* ²³*For you have been born again, not of perishable seed, but of imperishable, through the living and enduring word of God.* ²⁴*For,*
> *"All men are like grass,*
>   *and all their glory is like the flowers of the field;*
> *the grass withers and the flowers fall,*
>   ²⁵*but the word of the Lord stands forever."*
> *And this is the word that was preached to you.*

"Deep love" (1:22): Do we have this kind of love for our brothers and sisters? Is it a love that comes late to church and leaves the fellowship early, or one that comes to give and puts others first? Does it cross over to the other side of the road (Luke 10:31), or does it make every effort to keep all the saints on the narrow road? (Hebrews 3:12). Is it a pure love or a selfish love?

You will not find deep love in a false disciple, a false religion or a false church. It is made possible only because of rebirth, and sustained only through constant personal renewal (2 Corinthians 4:16) and deep, involved fellowship (Hebrews 10:24; Philippians 2). Jesus' life was all about people, and so are our lives, if we are really following him.

"Rebirth" (1:23): We were not reborn through perishable seed (human sperm), but through the seed, the word of God

(Luke 8:11), which is imperishable. This happens at baptism.
There is no other way to be reborn. The modern doctrine of
"pray Jesus into your heart" originated in the last century in
the United States; there is not a shred of evidence in the Bible
to support it! Don't be sentimental; people who have followed
the easy, man-made path to salvation are not right with God.
We need to interpret Scripture carefully, especially when it
concerns crucial issues like how to be saved.

Compare these three passages: 1 Peter 1:3, 1:23, and 3:21.
What do you see? Rebirth through the resurrection, rebirth
through [obeying] the word of God, and salvation by baptism
through the resurrection. The three passages are complemen-
tary, not contradictory. There is only one way to be saved: the
way the Bible says!

Since the Word preached to us is eternal, we are born again
and receive eternal life in the waters of baptism (John 3:5; Titus
3:5). Men are as ephemeral as the grass, but God's word en-
dures forever. Thus our salvation is solid; it is clinched. Our
persecutors will return to the dust they came from, biting it as
they go! Keeping this eternal perspective, we will truly enjoy
our salvation. For though we believe in realities invisible,
through faith in God we are invincible!

To his generation Peter might have said in our vernacular,
"Look, salvation is awesome! It's worth it, though it's constantly being tested—especially now in this time of persecution. Let's get a grip and let's get focused!" So—yes!—even in
such circumstances we can have life to the full. But we must
seek it and pursue it!

? What evidence is there that you have the kind of deep love for your brothers and
sisters that Peter describes? Is your love for others a pure love or a selfish love?
When do you see tendencies toward the second? How have you seen the power
of true love affect the lives of non-Christians?

9

In His Steps
1 PETER 2

Suffering is an integral part of following Jesus, sacrifices are part of our priesthood, and persecution is to be expected. This neatly sums up 1 Peter 2. But you aren't interested in a summary, or you would not be reading this book. You want to see it for yourself and to experience the life precious to Peter and precious to you, too, if you are following in Jesus' steps. This is the key to having life to the full.

> *¹Therefore, rid yourselves of all malice and all deceit, hypocrisy, envy, and slander of every kind. ²Like newborn babies, crave pure spiritual milk, so that by it you may grow up in your salvation, ³now that you have tasted that the Lord is good.*

In essence Peter pleads with us, "Since salvation is so awesome, get your heart right!" If we, as disciples, will do just these few things—be loving, open, consistent, humble and supportive—we will never fall away. We will make it to heaven, bringing along thirty, sixty or even a hundred others in our trains!

Are you craving pure spiritual milk? Is your appetite for spiritual food greater than that for physical food? The image of milk (see Hebrews 5) suggests there were many young ("baby") Christians in the churches of Asia Peter addressed. (Let's hope so!) Here are some simple questions you can ask yourself:

- Do you have a daily time of Bible study and prayer?
- If you have been a Christian a few years, have you read through the entire Bible yet?
- How quickly do you shake off your grogginess early in the morning when you think about your relationship with God and your mission?

- How often do you take notes during sermons? Do you especially write down life-changing insights?
- Does your enthusiasm for knowing God rub off on others?
- Do your non-Christian friends take you seriously when they see your passion and discipline to pray and know the Scriptures?
- What is your attitude towards reading suggested books outside the Bible? Are you slow or quick to dive in?
- Are you too proud to see yourself as a newborn babe in need of milk?

If you are slack in any of these areas, it may be an indication that you are self-satisfied and complacent. Since you have tasted how good the Lord is, cling to him and get serious about rising up to serve him in greater and greater ways!

? Which of the questions above are most challenging to you? In which of these areas have you made the most progress? Which of these issues might have the most impact on the entirety of your spiritual life?

4As you come to him, the living Stone—rejected by men but chosen by God and precious to him—5you also, like living stones, are being built into a spiritual house to be a holy priesthood, offering spiritual sacrifices acceptable to God through Jesus Christ. 6For in Scripture it says:
     "See, I lay a stone in Zion,
             a chosen and precious cornerstone,
     and the one who trusts in him
             will never be put to shame."
7Now to you who believe, this stone is precious. But to those who do not believe,
     "The stone the builders rejected
             has become the capstone,"
8and,
     "A stone that causes men to stumble
             and a rock that makes them fall."
They stumble because they disobey the message—which is also what they were destined for.

The "stone" theme is well illustrated in Isaiah and Psalms, a theme well familiar to OT readers. Jesus himself makes much of the theme in his own preaching, as does Paul. Check the cross-references in your Bible. After showing from the OT how Jesus is the Living Stone, arriving on our planet on schedule and being rejected on schedule, Peter continues to explain our "priesthood."

A priest, by definition, is holier than the common man and is called to sacrifice and mediate: He represents God to man and man to God, and he offers sacrifices for the forgiveness of sins. All Christians are called to the same two duties: sacrifice (personally) and mediation (bringing God and his word to man). In Protestant theology this is called the "priesthood of believers." Disciples have a priestly function! We are *all* ministers.

But Protestantism has betrayed its roots, returning instead to a quasi-Catholic "clergy-laity" system, where the ministers are often seen as more holy than lay people. The clergy-laity system in Christendom is flawed for three major reasons: it is elitist, it fosters a double-standard of commitment, and it's unbiblical. Consider some of the popular denominational titles current today:

- **"Father."** Jesus clearly told us to avoid this honorific title (Matthew 23:9).
- **"Pope."** Literally means "father." The papacy with its finery is far removed from the raw faith of the apostle Peter—who never claimed to be a pope!
- **"Pastor."** Occurs in most English Bibles only in Ephesians 4:11 as a concession to groups with "pastors." It is merely Latin for "shepherd," and interchangeable with "elder" (Acts 20; 1 Peter 5).
- **"Bishop."** Corruption of Greek *episkopos,* meaning "overseer," the position of elder. Whereas in the Bible the "bishop" was intimately familiar with his church (1 Peter 5), the modern bishop in his cathedral exercises ecclesiastical oversight over his "diocese" only at a distance.
- **"Priest."** Probably a corruption of *presbyteros,* Greek for "elder" or a confusion with the OT office. In the fourth century the church regressed into a fusion of paganism and Judaism, resulting later in full-blown Catholicism.
- **Female pastors.** Roundly rejected by the NT (see 1 Timothy 2; 1 Corinthians 14) but popular among born-again movements. Lack of strong male leadership encourages this.

• **"Monks"** and **"nuns."** Developed in second and third century as reaction to worldliness of the church and its "clergy." Error: Jesus said we are *in* the world but not *of* the world.

"Stumbling" (2:7): In OT times Jews stumbled because they lacked faith (Isaiah 8:14), and the same thing is happening all over again in Peter's day—and ours.

"Which is also what they were destined for" (2:8) means not that they were predestined to reject Jesus, but that people who reject the Living Stone are destined (bound) to fall.

> *⁹But you are a chosen people, a royal priesthood, a holy nation, a people belonging to God, that you may declare the praises of him who called you out of darkness into his wonderful light. ¹⁰Once you were not a people, but now you are the people of God; once you had not received mercy, but now you have received mercy.*

Just as Israel was given a universal mission (Exodus 19:6), we, too, declare God's praises. If we are cooling down in our evangelism, we are on the same slippery slope as Israel, forgetful of their calling, mission and responsibility to the nations. We sing the praises of restaurants, films, CDs and sports teams, why not declare the praises of God, his word and his church?

Once, says Peter, we had not received mercy, yet we crossed over from darkness to light when we received new birth into a living hope through baptism. Since there is no such thing as a little saved, every Christian knows when they repented and were baptized. There's a *specific* point in time.

> *¹¹Dear friends, I urge you, as aliens and strangers in the world, to abstain from sinful desires, which war against your soul. ¹²Live such good lives among the pagans that, though they accuse you of doing wrong, they may see your good deeds and glorify God on the day he visits us.*

As priests ready to sacrifice we must watch ourselves (Luke 17:3). Sinful desires are waging war against our soul, and the pagans are scrutinizing our lives, looking for a ray of hope, or perhaps hoping to catch us in some hypocrisy. They will glorify God and praise you, too, for your good example. Too many potential seekers are driven away by hypocrisy in the lives of disciples. Peter's hope is for the conversion of these onlooking outsiders (2:12).

? How do you disgrace God's name among the pagans? Are you unemployed or underemployed? Are you neglectful, late to work, slack or undisciplined? Do you lose your temper, harbor grudges or develop bad attitudes? Is your marriage exemplary? Is your residence untidy? Do you let your kids run wild?

> [13]*Submit yourselves for the Lord's sake to every authority instituted among men: whether to the king, as the supreme authority,* [14]*or to governors, who are sent by him to punish those who do wrong and to commend those who do right.* [15]*For it is God's will that by doing good you should silence the ignorant talk of foolish men.* [16]*Live as free men, but do not use your freedom as a cover-up for evil; live as servants of God.* [17]*Show proper respect to everyone: Love the brotherhood of believers, fear God, honor the king.*

Another area we, as disciples, are being watched in is our dealings with authorities, to whom we are called to submit— even if we don't like them! (prime minister, president, teacher, professor, bank clerk, traffic policeman, Internal Revenue Service...). Remember, the emperor in Peter's day, Nero, was *not* a "good" emperor. Submission only to people you like and agree with is not submission at all. For more on this, see Romans 13. (Of course, it goes without saying we should *not* obey when what is asked violates God's law or our conscience. See the example of Peter and John in Acts 5:29.)

A Word on Discipleship

Does the command to submit to authorities include disciplers, that is, men or women who give us spiritual input and call us to be disciples of Jesus? No, not in the same way that we must obey the authorities. True, all disciples are to submit to one another (Ephesians 5:21), and in this respect even husbands will need to show humility and submit to their wives (see Genesis 21:12!). In this way, we should absolutely submit to those who lead us. But disciplers are only friends, advisers, more spiritually mature persons who can coach us. If we are smart we will learn everything we can from them! And from many others, too (Proverbs 15:22). Now hopefully they're inspirational examples, but they are not infallible! However, God clearly works through people: This is a common teaching of the Bible. God's permitting someone to help us does not mean we should obey without thinking since we are each responsible for our own actions, but we should carefully consider their advice. Let us thank God for the people he has blessed us with in our lives and always be humble in our relationships with them.

? Do you see submission as a glorious principle or a galling burden? Is there anyone in your life—any person or any authority—to whom you do not show proper respect? How do others see your love for the brotherhood of believers?

> [18]*Slaves, submit yourselves to your masters with all respect, not only to those who are good and considerate, but also to those who are harsh. [19]For it is commendable if a man bears up under the pain of unjust suffering because he is conscious of God. [20]But how is it to your credit if you receive a beating for doing wrong and endure it? But if you suffer for doing good and you endure it, this is commendable before God.*

Often we suffer because of the insensitivity of others, in this case through the harshness of a master. Substitute the word "boss," "roommate," or even "leader" à la Gene Edwards' *Tale of Three Kings*. How do we normally react in such circumstances? And, as Peter asks, are we conscious of God? Sadly, in times of stress often the first thing to go is the Christian veneer.

Yet how much of our suffering is self-inflicted? Though God works through *all* types of suffering to test and refine our hearts, much of that suffering is brought on by our own stubbornness and foolishness, isn't it? But when we truly suffer for the gospel—and this is an integral part of the Christian walk (2 Timothy 3:12; Luke 6:22-23, 26)—God sees and will commend us at the appropriate time (see 1 Peter 5:6).

> [21]*To this you were called, because Christ suffered for you, leaving you an example, that you should follow in his steps.*

[22]*"He committed no sin,*
and no deceit was found in his mouth."

[23]*When they hurled their insults at him, he did not retaliate;*
when he suffered, he made no threats. Instead, he entrusted
himself to him who judges justly. [24]*He himself bore our sins in*
his body on the tree, so that we might die to sins and live for
righteousness; by his wounds you have been healed. [25]*For you*
were like sheep going astray, but now you have returned to
the Shepherd and Overseer of your souls.

"Suffering" (2:23): A good test of how closely we are following Jesus is how loudly we complain when asked to sacrifice. Since Jesus suffered the way he did, we have no excuse for shirking this demand of discipleship.

The cross gives two instructions: We must die to sins and we must live for righteousness (2:24). Avoidance of sin without discipleship makes a religious person; activity without purity makes a hypocrite and a liability to the cause. Jesus does not allow us the option of choosing which we prefer.

It may not be flattering to be called a sheep, but it is a constant analogy in the Bible for man and his tendency to wander. This being the true, we all need a shepherd! Jesus (like the elders of 1 Peter 5) is Shepherd and Overseer. Returning to our shepherd (who himself was also a sacrificial lamb) means we must be ready to sacrifice, walking *in his steps!* This lies at the heart of the gospel! And, when we do return, we will have life to the full.

? In what specific way is Peter saying we should follow in Christ's steps? How does following Christ change the way you look at suffering? How can suffering possibly fit with "life to the full"?

10

Semper Paratus
1 PETER 3

*S*emper Paratus: "Always prepared," is the official motto of the U.S. Coast Guard, as well as a near exact quote from 1 Peter 3:15 (Latin translation). For you more electrically minded readers, it could be rendered "ever-ready." You see, God values preparation because the alternative is usually panic. Peter felt the strain that tests relationships, which somehow sours the love of life we are meant to have. At this time, let's listen to his sound advice. He knows what he is talking about; and how to be prepared when the heat is on and time is short is the trick.

> *¹Wives, in the same way be submissive to your husbands so that, if any of them do not believe the word, they may be won over without words by the behavior of their wives, ²when they see the purity and reverence of your lives. ³Your beauty should not come from outward adornment, such as braided hair and the wearing of gold jewelry and fine clothes. ⁴Instead, it should be that of your inner self, the unfading beauty of a gentle and quiet spirit, which is of great worth in God's sight. ⁵For this is the way the holy women of the past who put their hope in God used to make themselves beautiful. They were submissive to their own husbands, ⁶like Sarah, who obeyed Abraham and called him her master. You are her daughters if you do what is right and do not give way to fear.*

Suffering increases pressure, and pressure strains relationships. At times like these, harmony is often forfeited. Peter, a man acquainted with suffering (like his Master), takes advantage of the moment to offer some practical advice.

The marriage relationship is a highly testing relationship. Pressure comes in many forms: not just persecution, but also busy times in the ministry, transitions in parenthood, sickness in the family, visits from in-laws, financial hardship, and changes in schedule. Little wonder non-Christians succumb to marital tensions and usually opt for the easy ways out: "peaceful" coexistence or divorce. How are we doing as married disciples? Do we let Satan win by sacrificing our marriage in the face of pressure?

The wives of non-Christian husbands may be the most tested disciples in the kingdom of God. What a temptation to despair, to retaliate or to simply to give up! Peter shares the secret of winning your mate over. Few women in this situation have the spirit of Sarah, and as a result, they hinder their husbands from becoming disciples. (Sometimes the situation is reversed, Christian husband with non-Christian wife, but this is less common.)

You are not married? You think the passage doesn't apply to you? Think again! There is a principle here that should be at work even before marriage and leading into marriage. Sisters, what is your attitude toward brothers who are in leadership in your life? Besides, most people will eventually marry. Why not start learning the attitude here ahead of time? It may improve your chances!

"Adornment" (3:3): Both men and women wore jewelry in biblical times without condemnation. Peter does not condemn jewelry, but urges that when this is the primary source of our attractiveness, our spirit is wrong.

> [7]*Husbands, in the same way be considerate as you live with your wives, and treat them with respect as the weaker partner and as heirs with you of the gracious gift of life, so that nothing will hinder your prayers.*

Submission is two-way in marriage (Ephesians 5:21, 22-24, 25-28, 33), and so is treating your spouse *kindly!* Lack of consideration impedes prayer, especially on the husband's part. Surely men will feel better, be more joyful, bear more fruit, give more in the fellowship and lead more spiritually when their most important human relationship is in good repair. Wondering why God isn't using you more? Why your children are slow to become Christians? Why the high-tension wires run through your sitting room? Look at your marriage, and look no further!

Peter deals with the women first, then the men. Rather than resent the six verses for women as opposed to only one verse for men, realize that he is putting more time and effort into helping the sisters. Peter spoke from his married experience (Mark 1:30). Even if you don't plan to get married anytime soon, check your attitude:

Some questions for wives/women:
- Do you nag?
- Do you make an effort to look attractive, both outwardly and inwardly?
- Do you resort to words and worldly means to win over your mate instead of doing it God's way?
- Do you fight for your rights, giving way to fear that you will lose the few rights you believe you have?
- Do you show respect for your husband and emphasize his strengths?

Some questions for husbands/men:
- Do you say negative things about your wife in front of others?
- How often do you compliment your wife, especially to others?
- When was the last time you took a second look at another woman?
- Are you generous in the amount of housework you do personally? Do you "delegate"? (Do you do anything?)
- Do you respect your wife for her spirituality and other strengths of character?

For both of you:
- Do you have another couple in your life you can openly share your lives, progress, setbacks, and even arguments with?
- Do you pray together regularly?
- Do your children have a fear of God?
- Are your family devotionals consistent?
- When outsiders visit your home and see your family, are they more likely to want to follow Christ, or less likely?

> *[8]Finally, all of you, live in harmony with one another; be sympathetic, love as brothers, be compassionate and humble. [9]Do not repay evil with evil or insult with insult, but with blessing, because to this you were called so that you may inherit a blessing. [10]For,*

> *"Whoever would love life*
> *   and see good days*
> *must keep his tongue from evil*
> *   and his lips from deceitful speech.*
> *[11]He must turn from evil and do good;*
> *   he must seek peace and pursue it.*
> *[12]For the eyes of the Lord are on the righteous*
> *   and his ears are attentive to their prayer,*
> *but the face of the Lord is against those who do evil."*

Harmony is so much lacking in this world, which is simply one of the consequences of sin and of the Fall (Genesis 3). Harmony is often in short supply even in the church. Peter exhorts us to live in peace with each other and with outsiders.

The quotation (3:10-12) is from Psalm 34:12-16. (By the way, Psalms is the most cited book from the OT. Originally the psalms were *sung* to stringed (plucked) instruments. In ancient Greek [pre-NT] *psallo* meant "to pluck or twang.") Peter, Jesus, and all the early disciples were intimately familiar with the book of Psalms, which gives us rich insights into the heart of God, as well as the heart of man.

? Write down two things you can do this week to contribute to greater harmony in
. relationships in your life. When is the last time you were insulted? How did you respond?

> *[13]Who is going to harm you if you are eager to do good? [14]But even if you should suffer for what is right, you are blessed. "Do not fear what they fear; do not be frightened." [15]But in your hearts set apart Christ as Lord. Always be prepared to give an answer to everyone who asks you to give the reason for the hope that you have. But do this with gentleness and respect, [16]keeping a clear conscience, so that those who speak maliciously against your good behavior in Christ may be ashamed of their slander.*

The context of this passage is continued evangelism in time of opposition.

"Fear" (3:14) is a clear and present danger facing disciples and not just in times of crisis. Of course there are all sorts of fears: "hydrophobia" (fear of water), "claustrophobia" (fear of closed spaces), "agoraphobia" (open spaces), "arachnophobia" (spiders), "acrophobia" (heights), "ochlophobia" (crowds), "xenophobia" (foreigners), and many more. What are your fears? Allow me to (half-jestingly) coin a few new words:

Religious Fears

1. "evangeliophobia"   fear of sharing your faith
2. "ecclesiophobia"   fear of church meetings
3. "diaconophobia"   fear of serving and menial work
4. "diocophobia"   fear of persecution
5. "bibliophobia"   fear of the Bible
6. "proseuchephobia"   fear of prayer
7. "theophobia"   fear of God
8. "staurophobia"   fear of crosses
9. "kriseophobia"   fear of judgment
10. "macrologophobia"   fear of long words!

Anyway, don't fear! God is with you! Psalm 27, John 14 and many other passages assure us that there is no need to fear. It is easy to give way to fear under persecution (3:14) and in relationships (3:6). When Christ is dwelling in our hearts by faith we overcome fear and the need to fear.

Since the text concerns continued evangelism in time of opposition, let's get practical. Effective evangelism is something we must learn from the masters. According to Simon bar Jonah (a.k.a. the apostle Peter), evangelism must be:

- *Christ-centered*: We preach Jesus Christ as Lord (2 Corinthians 4:5).
- *well-prepared*: No fumbling, stumbling or bumbling. We must know what we are talking about! (2 Timothy 2:15). However, eloquence is not a requirement (1 Corinthians 2:1-2).
- *gentle and respectful*: No place for heavy-handedness or self-righteousness!

- *non-retaliating*: We *will* be opposed. If we retaliate, we lose. Turn the other cheek (Matthew 5:39).
- *unhypocritical:* People will be eager to change when they see the awesome news supported (not contradicted) by our daily living.

? What fears do you have to overcome to be a great servant of Christ? How would you rate your own evangelism using the above list of criteria?

> *[17]It is better, if it is God's will, to suffer for doing good than for doing evil. [18]For Christ died for sins once for all, the righteous for the unrighteous, to bring you to God. He was put to death in the body but made alive by the Spirit, [19]through whom also he went and preached to the spirits in prison [20]who disobeyed long ago when God waited patiently in the days of Noah while the ark was being built. In it only a few people, eight in all, were saved through water, [21]and this water symbolizes baptism that now saves you also—not the removal of dirt from the body but the pledge of a good conscience toward God. It saves you by the resurrection of Jesus Christ, [22]who has gone into heaven and is at God's right hand—with angels, authorities and powers in submission to him.*

Here comes one of the most difficult passages in the NT. (And Peter said some of *Paul's* writings were difficult in 2 Peter 3:15!)

First, let's clear up some misconceptions about the Flood:

- The animals boarded in pairs, yes, but really by fours and fourteens (Genesis 7:2)—*not* "twosies."
- The Flood lasted not 40 days, but actually 375 days (Genesis 7:11, 8:14). The rains fell 40 days (Genesis 7:12).
- The ark did not land on Mount Ararat, but somewhere in the "mountains of Ararat" (Genesis 8:4).
- No "Nephilim" (Genesis 6:4) survived, because everyone besides the eight were drowned.
- The Bible is not the only ancient account of a worldwide deluge. There are scores of accounts in various cultures around the world.
- This is not just a myth. Jesus certainly seems to have seen the Flood as literal and historical, so we impugn Jesus'

intelligence when we insinuate that we know better than our Lord.

There are four major views on this difficult passage (1 Peter 3:19-20), each held by intelligent people:

1. Jesus gave those who died long ago a second chance to get right with God.

2. This was a victory proclamation. Jesus, after purchasing redemption, descended to Hades to proclaim his victory over death. The proclamation did not accomplish the salvation of its hearers.

3. This was the "harrowing of hell," the common medieval view, also affirmed in "The Apostles' Creed." Jesus "raided" the grave and led forth captives. This seems to be supported by Ephesians 4:6-10.

4. Jesus preached through the person of Noah. For some this finds support in other passages in 1- and 2 Peter.

Before examining the four views, we first need to put a few questions to the text:

• Exactly *who* are the spirits in prison?
• What *sort* of "preaching" was going on?
• *When* was this preaching taking place? In which generation did Christ preach?
• *How* did Christ preach?

As for the first question, about spirits, it is true angels were imprisoned according to 2 Peter 2:4. Many interpreters believe that the spirits are angels, or the angelic offspring of the illicit unions mentioned in Genesis 6:2. But can angels mate with humans? Doesn't this rather smack of Greco-Roman or Nordic mythology? (The "Nephilim" are certainly not the Titans of the Greeks or the Frost Giants of the Norse.) But if angels are awaiting final judgment, why couldn't deceased, unrighteous humans be in detention? At the day of judgment, heaven and hell will both become populated, filled. I see no hard and fast evidence that anyone has been sent to one place or the other *yet*. (See Acts 2:34.) Also, in Matthew 22:30 Jesus reminds us that angels do not marry. No "offspring" are ever mentioned in the Bible, so the above interpretation is suspect. As far as we know, in fact, the angels are *sexless*. Neither male nor female. It seems more likely that the "sons of God" in Genesis 6:2 are humans, whether the line of Seth (godly offspring) or human leaders (another view). For the line of Seth, see Genesis 4:25-26. For human rulers, see Psalm 82:6-7.

"The preaching:" Was it gospel preaching, for the purpose of saving the hearers, or was it some different type of preaching? The word for preacher or herald is *keryx*; the verb *kerysso* means "to preach or proclaim." (Usually *kerysso* refers to the preaching of a doctrine, topic or message, but it is nearly synonymous with *euangelidzo,* to proclaim, preach, preach the good news.)

Thirdly, we must decide when the preaching mentioned in 1 Peter 3:19 was taking place: whether in the time of Noah or in Jesus' time between his death and resurrection (the traditional view). Is this preaching *antediluvian* ("pre-Flood") or *anno domini* ("in time of Christ")? Both views are possible. If we decide that the preaching took place before Jesus' time, then we must ask how he preached "before his time." To put it another way, were they in prison *in order to* hear Jesus' preaching, or *because* they had refused to listen to it?

Evaluation

1. The doctrine of the "second chance," while attractive, must be rejected as completely unbiblical. The antediluvians' (those living before the Flood) chance to be saved was in Noah's time, not the first century A.D. If they got a second chance, maybe we get one, too. Why take the Great Commission so seriously if God is so easygoing? At first glance 1 Peter 4:6 seems to support this view, but soon the doctrine of "parole" or "purgatory" disqualifies itself (death is followed by judgment—Hebrews 9:27).

2. The victory proclamation view makes more sense. However, the reference to God's "patience" seems to mean that repentance was God's intent for the wicked men of Noah's day (see 2 Peter 3:9; Romans 2:4.): They and their descendants had over a century to repent, yet refused to! This preaching was just as likely evangelistic as proclamational. The NIV does well to translate *kerysso* as "preach."

3. The "harrowing" view, like view 2, explains what Jesus was doing between his death and resurrection, and seems to be a fairly natural reading of the passage. Jesus was killed and then in the Spirit accomplished his divine errand. But why

would he have needed to preach? A better question: Why would he have needed to *go* into the underworld? Perhaps the "lower, earthly regions" of Ephesians 4:9 means the earth in comparison with the heavenly regions, not the underworld.

4. I believe this preaching provided a chance to be saved, but in Noah's day. The key is found in the letters of Peter themselves. Although Christ never personally appeared in the OT, he operated through the Spirit at work in the prophets according to 1 Peter 1:10-12. If we accept that Noah was a prophet, and a preacher (*keryx*, according to 2 Peter 2:5!), why couldn't the Spirit of Christ have been working *through Noah* as he warned his generation, both by his actions and his words?

So how do we decide on the most plausible view? Let's step outside (outside the text) and settle this like men (and women) of God: by context! The context of the entire section 1 Peter 3:8-4:19 is *suffering.* Who suffered in the passage referring to Noah? How about Noah? He was willing to persevere for over one-hundred years while he built an ark that only his immediate family would appreciate. Like the Christians in Peter's day holding out the Word of life in Nero's reign, Noah was subject to slander and ridicule. Although his ark was big enough for a huge congregation, the faithful remnant who heeded his message numbered only eight. And after the suffering: exaltation—both for Noah and for disciples, if they stay faithful (1 Peter 5:10).

Like Christ, Noah was "righteous" (1 Peter 3:18; Genesis 6:9; 2 Peter 2:5). He preached, he suffered and he was vindicated. So it was with the readers of 1 Peter, and so it is in every generation of disciples.

Others may not agree with me—that doesn't mean they're necessarily wrong, and certainly doesn't cast aspersions on their integrity or salvation—but this is the view which best commends itself to me. You have to decide for yourself.

At any rate, disciples are in the minority on the earth. Don't be surprised! But you say, "Only *eight* out of Noah's generation?!" We are shocked—even offended—because we fail to appreciate the horror of sin, the lostness of man and the holiness of God.

On Baptism

Some of us are so used to plucking a few words out of verse 21 to talk about baptism that we totally miss Peter's imagery: The water in the days of Noah was that which lifted the ark and separated it from the sinful world. In the same way baptism lifts us upwards through the resurrection of Christ and separates us from the filth of the world. The Flood destroys the world, but brings the faithful few into a whole new world. Baptism, similarly, destroys the old sinful nature and brings us upward into a new life.

About the "conscience" (1 Peter 3:21), we read "...as an *appeal* to God for a good conscience" (NRSV, emphasis added). Some translations read "pledge of a good conscience" (NIV), but that is hardly the meaning of the original word (*eperotema*). Possible meanings in the Greek are "request" and "appeal." The only reason to translate it "pledge" is to obscure the connection of baptism with forgiveness of sins. You can't *pledge* to God something you don't yet have, but you can *appeal* to God for a good conscience, which God provides when your sins are washed away.

Finally, Peter speaks bluntly: "baptism saves you." That is what Peter explicitly says. Let theologians quibble, the truth speaks for itself. Certainly baptism without faith doesn't save you, and baptism without repentance doesn't save you. But when baptism is *into* Christ and done with faith and repentance, it saves you! So one can no more be saved without it than Noah and his family could have been brought into a clean new world without a flood and an ark.

Baptism is no source of boasting for us. It is of Christ. It connects us to Christ. It saves because of Christ and his death and resurrection. But precisely because it is *of* Christ, baptism saves us!

? How would you explain to someone that baptism saved you? What convictions did you have at your baptism that you want to carry with you forever?

11

Judgment Is Beginning
1 PETER 4

The Christian life takes both strength and stamina. Many men and women have the strength, but lack the stamina to keep going faithfully year after year. Why do people quit? Is it God's fault or their own? Peter assures us that if our attitude is *right*, we *will* make it. Because quitters never win, and winners never quit!

> *[1]Therefore, since Christ suffered in his body, arm yourselves also with the same attitude, because he who has suffered in his body is done with sin. [2]As a result, he does not live the rest of his earthly life for evil human desires, but rather for the will of God. [3]For you have spent enough time in the past doing what pagans choose to do—living in debauchery, lust, drunkenness, orgies, carousing and detestable idolatry. [4]They think it strange that you do not plunge with them into the same flood of dissipation, and they heap abuse on you. [5]But they will have to give account to him who is ready to judge the living and the dead.*

A willingness to suffer—that was Jesus' attitude, and Peter commands us to make it ours, too. We've been called to suffer (1 Peter 2:21). This isn't sadistic, killjoy or just suffering for suffering's sake: It is Christlike. We suffer not because we enjoy it, or because smiling is sinful, or because suffering is more spiritual, but because, in identifying with Christ, we shoulder a burden (Matthew 11:30) and take up a cross (Matthew 16:24) for the sake of *love*: God's love for us, our love for God and our love for others.

Many areas of our lives as disciples are governed by this perspective on suffering: in marriage, we must learn to surrender "rights"; persecution for our faith is normal, not rare (John 15:18); getting up in the morning always brings its own challenges (Proverbs 6:9-11); swimming upstream, shining as lights in the midst of darkness, sticking to the narrow road, with its sometimes precarious footing: all these things demand commitment, patience, energy—in short, an attitude of rejoicing in suffering.

Carousing and its cousins (4:4-5) come alive in our day! There many dens of darkness where people go to for no other purpose but sensual indulgence. How can I decide whether a certain place/activity is suitable for me? How are we to be *in* the world but not *of* the world? How can we associate with unbelievers and build friendships but not plunge with them into a flood of dissipation? Here are some questions we need to ask:

- Would Jesus go there? Would the Lord join in? (Usually this question settles it!)
- Will other Christians (especially young disciples) be edified by my participation, or potentially led into sin (Luke 17:1-3)?
- Does this help my credibility with non-Christians, the "watching world"? Check Ephesians 5:1-15!
- Is there *another* time or *another* activity that would be a better substitute for this one?

"Strange" harks back to "strangers" in 1 Peter 1:1. Morally speaking, Christians might as well have come from another world! The putrescent moral flood is the flood we must watch out for today; Peter is making a word play on the Flood of Noah.

? How did you feel about the questions above? What does your reaction say about your attitude toward being *in* the world but not *of* the world?

> *⁶For this is the reason the gospel was preached even to those who are now dead, so that they might be judged according to men in regard to the body, but live according to God in regard to the spirit.*

Gospel preached to the dead? Probably he is referring to the martyrs. Men judged them guilty (possibly of Nero's crimes) but they live spiritually. I do not think the "dead" here are "the spirits in prison" of 1 Peter 3:19, who had been placed in prison because of their disobedience, *not* because in the underworld they had reformed and were ready for "parole."

*[7]The end of all things is near. Therefore be clear minded
and self-controlled so that you can pray.*

The end of all things is near? Did Peter expect the end of
the world in his lifetime? Perhaps, but I think not. Just as we
may be nearer to death (our end) at some times than others
(close calls, near-death experiences, medical disasters) without being chronologically closer to death, so that the end of
the world may have been nearer, in a sense, simply because of
the terrible suffering of the Christians. The world did not end,
new generations were generated, yet all the while God has made
it clear that humans, to some extent, influence the time of the
end (2 Peter 3:12). What an incredible thought!

Once again, being "near death," or "close to being fired,"
or "on the brink of despair" does emphatically not mean that
soon thereafter a person will die, lose his job, or give up all
hope. It depends on how the word "near" is being used. Yet it
certainly is encouraging that when times are intense (as in 64
A.D.), the Lord is near (see Philippians 4:5).

Actually, there are many "ends" in the Bible. Here is only a
brief list:

- The end of Babylon at the hand of the Medes (Jeremiah
  51:13). Nations can be said to come to an end.
- The "day of the Lord" (Amos 5:18). Israel was taken into
  Assyrian captivity. Let me emphasize that this has nothing
  to do with the Judgment Day, but only the judgment of
  Israel in history through a foreign nation.
- The formal end of Judaism. The "last days" of Acts 2:17 are
  the final years of Judaism, between Pentecost and the
  destruction of Jerusalem some 40 years later. Matthew 10:22
  and 24:14 speak of the end of Israel as a nation and the
  destruction of Jerusalem with its temple. We may be living
  in the last days of human history, but we are not living in
  the last, final days of Judaism—which ended more than
  1900 years ago! Furthermore, the modern doctrine of the
  "end times" touted in best-selling religious books is
  completely without basis—based on conjecture, speculation
  and the worst kind of biblical interpretation and Scripture
  twisting.
- The end of the world, as in 2 Peter 3.

Once again, responsible interpretation will not jump to the conclusion that "feels" right; it's our responsibility and privilege to study the *whole* Bible and so understand biblical themes in the light of their biblical contexts. The oft-repeated claim that the early generations of Christianity, along with the apostles, expected the end at any moment, is difficult to prove.

> *[8]Above all, love each other deeply, because love covers over a multitude of sins. [9]Offer hospitality to one another without grumbling. [10]Each one should use whatever gift he has received to serve others, faithfully administering God's grace in its various forms. [11]If anyone speaks, he should do it as one speaking the very words of God. If anyone serves, he should do it with the strength God provides, so that in all things God may be praised through Jesus Christ. To him be the glory and the power for ever and ever. Amen.*

Hospitality is a duty and privilege of all Christians, especially men (scan the OT and read 1 Timothy 3:2, where it is a qualification for eldership).[1] There are also other gifts God expects us to use. There are gifts of speaking and gifts of serving. In the NT the most important gifts, according to 1 Corinthians 12 and Ephesians 4, are the teaching gifts. Every Christian has at least one gift, according to the NT (Romans 12:3-8, 1 Corinthians 12:1). To build up the body of Christ, we need to (1) identify them, (2) use them and (3) do it cheerfully.

Speaking the very words of God implies an attitude, not direct inspiration. God uses us, but that does not mean his imprimatur or mark of approval is on everything we say and do! Still, it is a great privilege to serve and to speak, whether in the pulpit, the children's ministry, a leaders' meeting or even a personal one-on-one Bible study.

? How are you doing in the area of hospitality? Who do you know who is a great example in this area? How can you imitate them? What gifts do you believe God has given you? What gift do you have that is being underused?

---

[1] For excellent and practical material on this vital topic see *The Fine Art of Hospitality*, Sheila Jones, et. al., eds., Discipleship Publications International, 1995.

> *12Dear friends, do not be surprised at the painful trial you are suffering, as though something strange were happening to you. 13But rejoice that you participate in the sufferings of Christ, so that you may be overjoyed when his glory is revealed. 14If you are insulted because of the name of Christ, you are blessed, for the Spirit of glory and of God rests on you. 15If you suffer, it should not be as a murderer or thief or any other kind of criminal, or even as a meddler. 16However, if you suffer as a Christian, do not be ashamed, but praise God that you bear that name.*

The verse reads: "Beloved, do not be surprised at the fiery ordeal that is taking place among you to test you" (NRSV). The "fiery ordeal" *(pyrosis pros peirasmon)* doubtless refers both to the refinement of faith (1 Peter 1:7), using a common biblical metaphor, and to the burning to death to which many Christian men and women in Rome were subjected under the brutal reign of Nero—news of which would have quickly traveled to Asia Minor.

How could Christians commit murder and theft? When we are being opposed, our first natural instinct is revenge upon, not prayer for, our enemies. In Jesus' day life was indeed cheap! Having your enemy killed was a relatively easy thing. Even today, in the Third World and places where knowledge of Christ and his teachings is minimal, *life is cheap.* Murder, infanticide and so forth are much more common in these lands.

The pagan world had many barbarous practices: abandonment of the elderly, abortion, child sacrifice, infanticide and exposure, the degradation of women, gladiatorial combat, cannibalism, slavery and many more social ills. In time, through the influence of Christianity, these shameful practices were phased out. Lately, however, with the increasing rejection of even the moral scaffolding of Christianity, many societies are sliding backwards into a pagan darkness that can be felt. (For further information, read *What If Jesus Had Never Been Born?* by D. James Kennedy.)

> *17For it is time for judgment to begin with the family of God; and if it begins with us, what will the outcome be for those who do not obey the gospel of God? 18And,*

"If it is hard for the righteous to be saved,
what will become of the ungodly and the sinner?"

[19]*So then, those who suffer according to God's will should commit themselves to their faithful Creator and continue to do good.*

Judgment has begun! This passage is not referring to the Judgment Day. This judgment comes through trials of various kinds (1 Peter 1:6). As hard as these trials are to endure even for Christians, how much less chance do unbelievers have. In times of testing, as well as at the Last Judgment, they will crumble or, more biblically, "crash" (Matthew 7:27). They lack the power of prayer, the support of the fellowship and the reinforcement and inspiration of gospel preaching. Their character, untrained in godliness, is often a push-over for Satan. Nor do they benefit from the pooled talents and mutual sharing of various gifts of the Spirit operating within the church.

Yes, the testing fires of judgment have begun (1 Corinthians 3:13). I am aware that there is a coming day when all will be tested, but how will unbelievers ever stand in that day if we believers scarcely (with difficulty) stand?

Wrap-up

Peter leaves us with one nourishing thought that should inspire us to action: the faithfulness of God. *Yes,* times will be tough. When the going gets tough, the tough get going. (At least according to Billy Ocean!) But don't forget God! Don't forget to entrust yourself to your Creator; you can count on him. When you are suffering, when you feel the weight of the rough cross on your back, it is no time to shut down, to withdraw into a shell or to take a break. Instead, remember Jesus, walk in his steps, keep going. It is no time to moan, groan, or feel all alone (because you aren't!), but it is time to keep going! Stamina!

? When is the last time you were insulted because of the name of Christ? What does it mean if this does not ever happen to you? How do you react to attacks on your faith and your life as a disciple? What is Peter calling you to do?

12

The Leader and the Lion
1 PETER 5

S ince judgment is already beginning, we need every strength and support we can get in order to make it to the end. God works to help us through people, and he has shown us in his word that he works through leaders. Leadership is service. Peter was not like most religious leaders, expecting to be served and demanding favors in exchange for leadership expertise. He, like his Master, was a servant-leader. Peter closes this magnificent letter with both love and solidarity as he identifies with churches and their elders.

> *[1]To the elders among you, I appeal as a fellow elder, a witness of Christ's sufferings and one who also will share in the glory to be revealed: [2]Be shepherds of God's flock that is under your care, serving as overseers—not because you must, but because you are willing, as God wants you to be; not greedy for money, but eager to serve; [3]not lording it over those entrusted to you, but being examples to the flock. [4]And when the Chief Shepherd appears, you will receive the crown of glory that will never fade away.*

God's plan is for churches to have evangelists and elders. Their jobs are to preach the Word (evangelists) and to protect the flock from lion and wolf (elders). The lives of biblical elders are characterized by a number of things:

- Marriage is upheld. Elders were required to be married (1 Timothy 3:2, 4-5), as Peter was (see Mark 1:30). Celibacy is not a spiritual requirement. (See 1 Timothy 4:1 and following.)
- Family is affirmed. The elder must be an exemplary family man and leader.
- They inspire by relationship rather than by position. They *care* for the flock. Far from the mercenary clergymen of

our day, these elders really cared for the men and women in their charge.

- An elder is Christlike, following the lead of Jesus Christ, who himself was the Good Shepherd (John 10) and is also the "Chief Shepherd" (1 Peter 5:4; Hebrews 13:20).
- Elders could be paid (1 Peter 5:2; see also 1 Timothy 5:17-18). Some elders serve full-time, while others are part-time, holding jobs in the "secular" world.
- "Those who are older" (1 Peter 5:5) are elders. The Mormons are wrong; a 19-year-old is too young! Yet not all "elders" are *elders*, since age isn't the only qualification.
- The crown: Having served well, elders attain a "crown of glory," which never fades (unlike the laurel wreath athletic champions vied for), treasure in heaven! The role of elder is a high office in the kingdom of God. It has been said that you can rise up and become an evangelist in a few years; becoming an elder requires a lifetime of qualification.

⁵Young men, in the same way be submissive to those who are older. All of you, clothe yourselves with humility toward one another, because,

"God opposes the proud
but gives grace to the humble."

⁶Humble yourselves, therefore, under God's mighty hand, that he may lift you up in due time.

Pride is such a dangerous thing! The oft quoted proverb above (Proverbs 3:34) reminds us of the real issue when disciples are having difficulty submitting to leadership.

In times of opposition, the proud and egotistical are often the first to compromise, the first to be duped by the invective of the critics and the first to fall away. Younger disciples are urged to be humble before their elders, just as the elders have been urged to be humble servants towards the younger. It is always better to humble yourself before God has to put you in circumstances that humble you. And remember, God's timing is different from ours. If you don't see yourself being lifted up here, you will be in heaven.

[7]Cast all your anxiety on him because he cares for you.

God begs us to give our anxieties to him! See the heart of God, a God who does not want any of his precious children to be weighed down by worry or sin. Those who do not pray become prey—prey for Satan.

? How does pride most often show up in your life? How strong is your hatred of it? What anxiety do you have today that needs to be cast on Jesus Christ? How do you do that?

> *[8]Be self-controlled and alert. Your enemy the devil prowls around like a roaring lion looking for someone to devour. [9]Resist him, standing firm in the faith, because you know that your brothers throughout the world are undergoing the same kind of sufferings.*
>
> *[10]And the God of all grace, who called you to his eternal glory in Christ, after you have suffered a little while, will himself restore you and make you strong, firm and steadfast. [11]To him be the power for ever and ever. Amen.*

Satan, like a stalking lion, preys on the weak: the lustful, the lazy, the irresponsible, the idle, the stingy, the proud, the unforgiving, latecomers, those who flirt with sin...and, above all, those who are not "self-controlled and alert."[1]

We are not alone in our struggle. Amen! But there is more good news: the suffering is temporary! "This too will pass." No, you were not just born at an unlucky time; God had planned for your faith to be refined in the fires of suffering.

Finally, suffering is normal, yet (good news!) it's only temporary. Peter provides us with four examples to follow in the face of suffering: Jesus Christ (chapter 2), Noah (chapter 3), the martyrs (chapter 4) and brothers around the world (chapter 5).

> *[12]With the help of Silas, whom I regard as a faithful brother, I have written to you briefly, encouraging you and testifying that this is the true grace of God. Stand fast in it.*

---

[1] Watch for a new book on the roaring lion who seeks to devour us that my friend Mike Taliaffero is writing after his many years in Africa. It is expected to be released in 1996 by Discipleship Publications International.

[13]She who is in Babylon, chosen together with you, sends you her greetings, and so does my son Mark. [14]Greet one another with a kiss of love.
Peace to all of you who are in Christ.

Silas (or Silvanus, his full name) served as Peter's secretary. It was common practice in the ancient world to dictate to a scribe, even when the sender of the letter was literate. The technical word for this person is *amanuensis*. This also explains the excellent mastery of Greek 1 Peter displays and the impressive vocabulary of 2 Peter; scholars agree that Aramaic-speaking Peter certainly benefited from his Greek *amanuensis*.

"Babylon," (5:13) as in the book of Revelation, is Rome. The word "Babylon" was a symbol of corrupt, ungodly political power. (Yes, there was a colony of Jews still in existence at Babylon in the first century, but there is no evidence of Christianity there.) Most commentators agree that "she" refers to a sister church (see parallel in 2 John 1).

Mark (5:13) is clearly close to the apostle. The relationship was well established in Peter's lifetime, no second-century fiction as some liberal scholars assert. Mark went to Rome, sat at the feet of Peter and committed his preaching to words: the gospel of Mark. Thus Peter left us with three literary productions: 1 Peter, 2 Peter and Mark.

Digression: The Holy Kiss

The kiss (5:14): Is it just cultural, or binding today? Yes! The outward form of the expression is cultural, yet the inner content is absolutely God's will for human relationships: touch, affection, expressiveness.

When I started going to religious meetings, besides the free food, one thing that attracted me was the so-called holy kiss. ("What an opportunity!" I thought.) But, biblically the kiss was typically between members of the same sex! (Genesis 33:4, for instance.)

In many places the kiss is still a standard greeting: France, the Middle East and North America, for example. In France, men kiss women (on both cheeks), women kiss men, and women even kiss women. Rarer is the man kissing a man! In the Middle East, apart from family relations, men kiss men and women kiss women. This was likely the kiss to which Peter refers (Song of Songs 8:1). In North America, kissing is usually more restricted to family and romantic contexts, but even then, men kiss women and vice versa.

In deciding how best to greet someone, the 1 Corinthians 9 principle comes into play: "becoming all things to all men." We must ask ourselves what promotes the gospel and what hinders it? (See also 1 Corinthians 10:32-33.) So, let's greet our Christian brothers and sisters *affectionately*. That doesn't necessarily mean we have to kiss one another. It all depends on what part of the world we are in!

"Peace" (5:14) is for those in Christ. Yes, we want the whole world to have peace, yet we realize this is a pipe dream unless people become disciples. As Isaiah put it, "There is no peace for the wicked" (Isaiah 48:22, 57:21). True peace is found only in doing God's will. As David put it, "My soul finds rest in God alone" (Psalm 62:1). This is life to the full.

? How do you see the roaring lion working to devour you? Your closest friends and family? Why does Peter believe we do not have to cower or give up in the face of such a fierce enemy? What is the lesson of the "holy kiss" for you personally? How much are you known in the fellowship for your affection?

Recommended:

Refined by Fire, Gordon Ferguson, available from Discipleship Publications International. Booklet and tape series on 1-2 Peter.

13

The Dark Ages
2 PETER

Only weeks or months before his death, Peter had a burden on his heart. Like Moses in OT times (Deuteronomy 31:16), he knew Satan would strike hard in the near future and that only a remnant would survive. Such falling away on a large scale is called "apostasy," from the Greek *apostasia*, meaning "rebellion or abandonment." Since it was to forewarn and protect the church of Christ from apostasy that Peter penned his second powerful epistle, this is a good time to get an overview of church history through the ages.

Core Principles

Following are three points to keep in mind when approaching the involved subject of church history: apostasy is possible, predicted, and yet preventable.

Possible in Principle

While Matthew 28:20 assures us God will be with us in the mission, it cannot be construed as a guarantee that the church can never die out. A careful look at Matthew 16:18 shows the same thing: No obstacle can stop the church on the march. But when the people of God stop acting like the people of God—watch out!

2 Chronicles 15:2-3, a passage describing the "dark ages" of the OT, assures us that the Lord is with us "when we are with him." Moreover, it is possible that, due to apostasy, the supposed people of God can remain without God and the truth "for a long time." So, apostasy is possible in principle, for any generation—and a probability for any generation careless with its commitment.

Predicted in Scripture

The most shocking development in church history must surely be the great falling away. Such an epic historical event is, not surprisingly, revealed in advance to God's inspired speakers and writers (Amos 3:7). For example, Moses foretold the imminent apostasy of Israel in Deuteronomy 28. (The history of Israel (OT) isn't the most encouraging reading material!)

Similarly, in Matthew 24:12 Jesus speaks about his generation, saying that "the love of most will grow cold." In Matthew 24:34 he assures us that everything in this discourse would be fulfilled in their generation, culminating in the physical destruction of Jerusalem, as the passage makes clear. These are somber words, yet the word of God is clear: The majority of Christians in the generation 31-70 A.D. would *not* stay *hot*.

2 Peter 2:1-3 repeats the prophecy of Jesus and applies it to the late first and following centuries. *Why* would the people defect? Greed and gullibility are two factors indicated by Peter. *When* would this happen? Gradually, I believe, yet certainly by the fifth century, spiritual chaos reigned.

Preventable with Determination

Apostasy is preventable, and we have an advantage in having the history both of Israel and the Christian church to steer us between the rocks that could shipwreck our faith: as individuals, as congregations and as a movement. We must make a decision, as Joshua's generation made in Joshua 24. It will also take our personal involvement in the fellowship, not just concern for friends but also for those we have never met (Colossians 1:28-2:1). When lukewarmness does creep in, we will have to be earnest, repent, and get hot, letting Jesus back into our hearts (Revelation 3:14-22). Those who choose not be hot and love the Lord (John 14:15, 24) are, in fact, under a curse (1 Corinthians 16:22)! Perhaps more than anything else, we will have to strive supremely to keep the unity of the Spirit (Ephesians 4:3). Defeat is avoidable, and while the victory is not clinched, it is certain if we are committed to these things. So stay positive and prayerful!

Compact Overview

Christians need to have the big picture of Bible history, and also the big picture of church history. Nearly 2,000 years of church history is a little hard to digest in one sitting, so the reader will appreciate the compact overview. There are six historical phases we can distinguish.

Committed Church

The faith and commitment of New Testament times continued through the first and second centuries, urged on by the fires of persecution. Though far from perfect as a church, the early disciples were not far from the Lord Jesus in terms of radical commitment.

Cooling Off

As superstition, Judaism and paganism filtered into the church, many exchanged their vibrant faith for a more comfortable "religion." This period extended from around the third century, when popular Christianity drifted into many interesting innovations, to the late fourth century, after the cessation of persecution and legalization of Christianity. It is also during this time that many left the church for the desert. Protesting the growing worldliness of people and leaders, monks separate themselves from the mainstream of Christianity.

Catholic

The Emperor Constantine mediated in Christian doctrinal disputes as early as 325 A.D. In 381 Christianity became the official religion of the empire. In the coming Holy Roman Empire, church and state were essentially fused into one. Millions of pagans were "converted," the standard of commitment plummeted and all the abuses of the Middle Ages were just waiting to happen.

The Catholic period lasted from late fourth/early fifth to the early sixteenth century. Attempts at reform were systematically squelched, sometimes with force, as in the Inquisition (thirteenth century onwards), through which some 30,000 men and women protesting error were tortured and executed.

Major errors: the Catholic church became the authority instead of Bible; the church and state became one instead of remaining separated; and instead of holding to the gospel, leaders allowed local superstitions to blend into the syncretistic, synthetic, Catholic religion.

Reformation

Starting with Martin Luther (1517), the reformers tried at first to clean up the Roman Catholic Church, then ended up clearing out altogether. This sixteenth-century movement was a long-awaited spiritual revolution. The Bible was brought to the common man in his own language (a major chief contribution of the Reformation). At last freed from the shackles of tradition, men and women were free to read and follow the Bible. Protestantism was born; but did they go far enough? Within a generation, the Reformation movement was hopelessly fragmented. A new beginning was desperately needed.

Restoration

With seeds in the Reformation and a wide following among those disaffected with stale, denominational Christianity, a restoration movement (with the goal of "restoring NT Christianity") gained momentum on both sides of the Atlantic, especially in the nineteenth century. Shedding sectarian labels, followers called themselves "Christians" or "disciples" only. This movement emphasized: personal Bible study, elimination of clergy-laity distinction, names like "Christians" and "disciples," weekly communion, immersion baptism and congregational elderships.

The Restoration Movement, divided first over petty issues like *instrumental music* and *missionary societies* and later over a host of other issues, lost not only its credibility but also its impetus. One branch of the movement became ecumenical; the other legalistic with both wings losing strength and numbers. Certain externals were "restored" but often the heart of biblical discipleship was not.

Realization

Just as the Restoration Movement sought to make up for the shortcomings of the Reformation, so in recent times a number of problems with the Restoration Movement have been recognized giving rise to a new and forceful movement that is spreading around the world at this hour.

In contrast to the Restoration Movement, every member is called to be a (committed, evangelistic) disciple. In keeping with this, the planting of new churches has replaced the old practice of cultivating a core group within existing churches. Finally, true disciples have committed themselves to world evangelization as soon as humanly (and divinely) possible.

Compact Church History

31	Church founded in Jerusalem.
70	Romans destroy Jerusalem; Christianity 100% separate from Judaism; NT completed
232	Earliest church building known to archaeology; clergy-laity separation.
381	Christianity becomes official religion of Roman Empire; standards decline.
400	Infant baptism common; original sin; predestination. *Dark Ages* begin.
606	Boniface III claims as pope to be sole head of all Christians.
1517	Luther launches Reformation in Germany.
1546	Counter-Reformation: Council of Trent brings Apocrypha into Bible.
1810	Restoration gathers steam.
1995	Present day: A worldwide movement calling men and women to be disciples with an evangelistic emphasis.

Prophets False and True

With all these things in mind, the reader will appreciate the many parallels between church history and the history of God's people in the OT. Peter stingingly, scathingly exposes the false prophets gaining ground in his day. For the record, let's consider the narrowness of the road from a biblical point of view.

What we see in our examination of church history is that most clergy are actually, as in Jesus' day, "the blind leading the blind." Now a blind prophet will necessarily also be a false prophet, since you can't *accidentally* teach someone the gospel. They have eyes to see, and they claim to see, but in fact do not see.

Another recurring theme is the outnumbering of the true prophets by the false prophets. Traditional religion, the establishment, the majority, is virtually always corrupt, and so the man or woman of God goes head-to-head against the false teacher. Two examples of this are the showdown on Mount Carmel (1 Kings 18), and the confrontation between Micaiah and Ahab (1 Kings 22).

As disciples of Jesus Christ we are called to a prophetic role (although we are not "inspired prophets" in the biblical sense). This being the case, we must decide to be true prophets who take opposition instead of false prophets who avoid it. (See Luke 6:22-23, 26.) Suffering has always been the mark of the true servant of God. (Take another look at Paul's defense of his ministry in 2 Corinthians, especially chapter 11.) The false prophets seek at all costs to avoid persecution (Galatians 6:12).

It's not just that the false prophets teach error; they fail to teach the truth, to expose sin and call to righteousness. Their standards are simply too low. Lamentations 2:14 is scathing indictment of false prophets. Consider the following illustrations of these principles:

The Time of Noah

Noah was a true prophet and "preacher of righteousness" (2 Peter 2:5), yet he was the only one in his day! Whatever the world population might have been, eight persons is a very small sliver of a percent that were saved. Remember, Peter selects Noah as an example for us today, both in 1 Peter 3 and 2 Peter 2).

The Time of Elijah

In Elijah's day there were 7,000 saved, with 850 false prophets. Israel's population at that time was probably several million; you work out the percentage! Elijah thought he was more outnumbered than he really was, and God came to encourage him (1 Kings 19).

The Time of Jesus

Jesus' day was no more righteous than any other time in the flow of OT history! Very few Pharisees and Sadducees were followers of Jesus, though there was the odd exception, like Nicodemus. (There were around 7,000 of these "clergymen" in Israel at the time.)

Today

Is our generation any more righteous than Jesus'? Than Elijah's? Noah's? Let's be realistic! When Jesus talks about the narrow road (Matthew 7:13), he means it! So how should we feel about all this? Two perspectives on salvation and heaven are spiritual, and both are easily proven from the Scriptures:

- *Few people will be saved,* percentage-wise. The overwhelming majority will go to destruction. Don't be surprised, don't back down and don't apologize. Rather, state clearly that the sorry state of affairs is a *disgrace!*
- *Heaven will be filled.* A stupendously enormous crowd will experience it. In absolute terms (not relative) the number of the saved will be impressive indeed! Encourage each other with this news.

In short, the apostasy predicted by Peter and others did happen. We see the chilling words of 2 Peter 2 come to life: rebellion and defection on a massive scale! Yet there is no reason it has to happen again in our day. That is, if we learn from history.

Lessons from History for Today

Many lessons can be culled from the annals of church history. If we are humble and wise enough to learn them, we will certainly evangelize our world more rapidly and effectively than if we choose to ignore what God has made clear: When people have followed the Word, the gospel has spread and taken root; where they have departed onto an unscriptural path, chaos has ensued. Following are a few lessons to be learned.

I. The Bible is the ultimate authority.

Never tell people, "Stop asking questions; just believe." That is very dangerous! Every single member must be studying the Word *daily.* We must always aim to keep standards of biblical education for full-time ministry workers high—not necessarily a seminary education, but an effective program for equipping ministers. No blind faith!

II. False teaching is dangerous.

Every book of the NT warns us of the peril of false teaching, and, while showing flexibility and grace, we should at all times be on our guard against the "yeast" which could leaven any part of the church of God in an unhealthy manner (Matthew 16:12). Moreover, false doctrine (literally, "unhealthy teaching") is a partner to tolerated sin. We all must stay on the cutting edge spiritually.

III. The church should stay out of politics.

There are very few occasions (in Western society) when a church will need to address a political issue head-on. A system of checks and balances will virtually remove the temptation to political or financial corruption. The abuses of the Middle Ages could repeat themselves if we are not careful. We must not risk our spiritual integrity by becoming obligated in any way to political authorities—apart from, of course, payment of taxes and observation of the laws of the land.

IV. Cooperation among congregations is crucial.

Just as the early congregations were in communication by visits and letters, we too must practice communication and cooperation excellently. Leaders must be in contact and in harmony (as were Peter and Paul—Galatians 2). On occasion, conferences may even need to be convened to address issues of importance to the whole brotherhood, as in the Jerusalem Council of Acts 15.

V. The clergy-laity system is unbiblical.

As long as there are leaders, there will be the human tendency to rationalize discipleship into two standards of commitment: disciple and "Christian," participant and spectator, clergy and laity. We must watch out! The path of least resistance is the path to hell.

VI. We must never think we have fully arrived!

We must never assume we have fully arrived, either as a movement or individually. Arrogance of this sort is fatal. In addition to the mathematical improbability of having recovered every biblical teaching in perfect balance, there are some practical considerations. For one, if you're right on every issue, you can never change your mind! And yet we do all the time. Second, everyone becomes the "enemy," with heresy lurking in every corner. Third, God won't be able to teach you anything new! Spiritual growth stagnates. Obviously, this is a description of centuries of ecclesiastical history—centuries we care not and dare not to repeat!

So let's learn the lessons of history. Peter warned us of the perils and made every effort to stave off as much of the false teaching as possible. Thus his second letter focuses on *knowledge*. He shows us in 2 Peter both the importance and the relevance of church history for the church universal and our own personal commitment:

Chapter 1: Grace and growth come only through the knowledge of God.

Chapter 2: Twisted gospels and twisted lives characterize the false teachers.

Chapter 3: Fear God and further your knowledge of him, and you'll never fall away.

Behold one of the most colorful letters in the entire New Testament!

? Why do you need to know the basic lessons of church history? What is dangerous about not paying attention to what has gone before us? Why is no movement for God ever immune from the danger of apostasy?

Recommended:

Prepared to Answer, Gordon Ferguson, available from Discipleship Publications International. Handy overview of church history and denominational doctrines.

14

Light Overcomes Darkness
2 PETER 1

Peter warned us of the peril of false doctrine and attempted to stave off false teaching as much as possible. Apostasy came, but the light kept shining. For light overcomes darkness, and it is up to us to carry the torch. That's why *knowledge* is really the theme of his second letter. Let our exegesis begin!

> *¹Simon Peter, a servant and apostle of Jesus Christ,*
> *To those who through the righteousness of our God and*
> *Savior Jesus Christ have received a faith as precious as ours:*
> *²Grace and peace be yours in abundance through the knowl-*
> *edge of God and of Jesus our Lord.*

Notice the word order. Simon Peter is first a servant, and second an apostle. Peter had learned a great deal about Christlike leadership over the years.

Notice also Peter's assertion of the divinity of Christ. (Other passages emphasizing this are John 1:1, Romans 9:5, Titus 2:13 and Hebrews 1:8, to mention just a few.) Jehovah's Witnesses are dead wrong when they corrupt John 1:1 to make it say "the Word was a god." In fact the same construction (*theos*, "god" without the definite article) appears in four other verses in John 1 (1:6, 1:12, 1:13, 1:18), and each time the Jehovah's Witnesses *New World Bible* "translators" render the construction "God." But obviously attacks on Jesus' deity are as old as Jesus' original claim (see John 10:30-33).

Peter is on the offensive right from the start, going after false teachers who attack the deity of Christ, the miraculous claims of Christ, the sovereignty of Christ, and the "second coming" of Christ (more on this in Chapter 16 of this book).

Grace and peace come through a correct spiritual knowledge of God, which accepts Jesus as Lord: This is the theme of 2 Peter.

> *[3]His divine power has given us everything we need for life and godliness through our knowledge of him who called us by his own glory and goodness. [4]Through these he has given us his very great and precious promises, so that through them you may participate in the divine nature and escape the corruption in the world caused by evil desires.*

Since his divine power has given us everything we need through our knowledge of Christ, why listen to other (false) teachers? Who needs them? We already have all we need through the Scriptures; we are spiritually filled, not starving. Only a glutton would be enticed with dessert when he is already full!

We don't call ourselves by our *own* glory and goodness; this is God's initiative and all credit for our salvation belongs to him! The "promises of God" are many, and this topic makes for great personal Bible study. For example, consider Matthew 28:20, John 14:12 and 1 Corinthians 10:13, just for starters.

"Participating in the divine nature" (1:4) is not some esoteric experience available only to the mystics. It does involve being filled with the Spirit (Ephesians 5:18), but just as importantly it involves following in Jesus' steps, thereby identifying with him (1 John 2:6). But there is more to it than sharing in Jesus' divinity; we actually "escape the corruption of the world." Peter made the same plea in Acts 2:40. (A similar coupling of purity with righteous living is found in James 1:27.)

Are you escaping the corruption of the world, or does it still hold some claim on you? Consider James 4:4 and 1 John 2:15-17, and realize that the false teachers of 2 Peter 2 had either never escaped it or had escaped it and then had fallen away, entangled and overcome by the lust of the world. Keep in mind that false teaching and immorality (corruption on all sorts of levels) go hand in hand. Corruption has its roots in evil desires and only Christ overcomes them. No other religion will do. For example, both Buddhism and Christianity admit that the world is corrupt. In Buddhism, a passive religion, one strives to extinguish *all* desire; in Christianity we aim to extinguish only the *evil* ones. Passion (the right sort) is good. With this in view, spiritual stagnation is fatal; spiritual growth is imperative!

? How do you see yourself as "participating in the divine nature"? How does that
  •   need to affect your self-image? How does that help you in the battle against sin?

> *5For this very reason, make every effort to add to your faith goodness; and to goodness, knowledge; 6and to knowledge, self-control; and to self-control, perseverance; and to perseverance, godliness; 7and to godliness, brotherly kindness; and to brotherly kindness, love. 8For if you possess these qualities in increasing measure, they will keep you from being ineffective and unproductive in your knowledge of our Lord Jesus Christ.*

This list is not a sequence of progressive virtues, and it's doubtful Peter meant it to be taken that way. Still, each quality is vital to spiritual health. And now, a test:

Personal Spiritual Growth Assessment

Faith (pistis)
We all start the Christian walk with faith, but is yours *growing?* Is your conviction strong? Do you feel uneasy about the "narrow road," or do you take a stand that it is the only road to heaven? What sorts of studying and praying are you doing to be nearer to God? Jesus was often amazed at the disciples' lack of faith. Let us, rather, impress him with our great faith!

Goodness, virtue (arete)
"Goodness" is not an attribute of the mythical "good moral person" of common parlance. The good person, like the Samaritan (Luke 10), actively seeks opportunities to help others. He or she is good not just when others are watching, but in private as well, and is far more concerned with virtue than with possible rewards or penalties (Colossians 3:22).

Knowledge (gnosis)
How is your knowledge and whom is it benefiting? Knowledge of God, his word; human nature, your own strengths and limitations; about current events, the worldwide discipling

movement; about your friends, spouse, children...and on and on. The point is not just to pile up knowledge, but to teach and help others! (Hebrews 5:11-14)

Self-control (enkrateia)
God's Spirit is a spirit of self-discipline. The Spirit teaches us to control our thoughts, tongues, desires, appetites and schedules. Is your life in control, or out of control? How are your New Year's resolutions going? A *disciple* without *discipline* is a walking contradiction!

Perseverance, endurance (hupomone)
How is your spiritual stamina? Do you have fits and starts? Do you work for a while then reward yourself too soon with a rest, losing your momentum? Are you like the Israelites in the desert (a complaining spirit)? Do you give up easily? Remember, "Winners never quit, and quitters never win."

Godliness, piety (eusebeia)
Is your life reverent? Is the Spirit conquering flesh on a daily basis (Galatians 5:16-18)? Are you easily distracted at church, or do you set a great example of being focused? Does anyone (apart from your enemies) doubt your spirituality, your godliness, your integrity or your character? How about your friends at work? Your wife? Your husband? Your fellow mission group members? Do you joke around *too* much?

Brotherly kindness (philadelphia)
It's one thing to have the truth and try to teach others; it's another thing to be tender, gentle and kind. We must speak the truth, yet in love (Ephesians 4:15, 25). We must teach others firmly, yet patiently (2 Timothy 2:23-26). We take responsibility for training other disciples to be more godly, yet consistently encouraging them (Hebrews 3:12-13). It has been said, "Be right, speak the truth, be nice—and in that order!"

Love (agape)
Finally Peter mentions the greatest of the virtues, *love*. Without this we are only "resounding gongs or clanging cymbals" (1 Corinthians 13:1). Loud Amen!s, seemingly zealous responses and much hoopla and hype are poor whitewash for

a dead heart. Jesus was who he was and accomplished what he
did because of *love*.

Self-rating

Rate yourself on a scale of 1 (low) to 5 (high) for each virtue,
then total your score:

Faith	1	2	3	4	5
Goodness	1	2	3	4	5
Knowledge	1	2	3	4	5
Self-control	1	2	3	4	5
Perseverance	1	2	3	4	5
Godliness	1	2	3	4	5
Brotherly kindness	1	2	3	4	5
Love	1	2	3	4	5

Scoring: 8-15 = Either you're a wicked sinner *or* you have
                 terribly low self-esteem!
          16-23 = Keep growing as a disciple.
          24-31 = You're doing well; focus on strengthening
                 the weak areas!
          32-39 = You're hot: put a veil over your face! (2
                 Corinthians 3:13)
             40 = You definitely *lie*. (See Revelation 21:8; Prov-
                 erbs 16:18.)

"Increasing measure" means simply that we are growing
stronger spiritually with each year that passes. Sometimes we
attempt to measure our growth too often and lose the real
picture of our progress. Checking your progress every few
months will be more encouraging than doing it every week.
For instance, someone trying to diet had best not step on the
scales every day—temporary fluctuations could cause unnecessary discouragement. "A watched pot never boils."

Peter's promise, like that of John 15:1-17, is simple: grow
spiritually and effectiveness is guaranteed. See, it's not com-
plicated! Most of the Christian faith is like that. The rules are
simple, the commands are not burdensome, the yoke is easy,
the burden is light.

⁹But if anyone does not have them, he is nearsighted and blind, and has forgotten that he has been cleansed from his past sins.

By the way, are you shortsighted and blind? Have you forgotten that you are cleansed? That you are a son or daughter of God? (Because you are!—1 John 3:1.) Have you forgotten your attitude of gratitude?

¹⁰Therefore, my brothers, be all the more eager to make your calling and election sure. For if you do these things, you will never fall, ¹¹and you will receive a rich welcome into the eternal kingdom of our Lord and Savior Jesus Christ.

We cannot earn our salvation, but we must be eager to let the grace of God do its work in our lives, thus producing evidence that our calling and election are real. "You will never fall" if you take Peter's admonition to heart. You may fall down occasionally, but you will not fall *away*! This encouraging fact he repeats in 2 Peter 3:17. Yes, our position is secure, providing we stay close to God. Stay under the shelter, and you need not fear the thunderstorm.

"A rich welcome"—what a reward! *Into* the eternal kingdom? Aren't we already in the kingdom? Yes, since Jesus is our King, and we live in his realm, we are in the kingdom. But absolutely not in the same way we will be at that last, great day! Have you noticed how very little detail the Bible gives us about heaven? I think human words would spoil it. They would fail to capture the magnificence, the awesomeness.

Heaven is something we instinctively long for. If it were not real, why would we have such a strong appetite for the spiritual? (See Ecclesiastes 3:11.) Every appetite in a human being has a corresponding fulfillment: sleep, food, drink etc. There is a heaven the other side of the grave: our extremely strong longing for it points to its existence.

? How often do you think about the rich welcome that you will have into your heavenly home? When are times when this thought would be most powerful and helpful?

¹²So I will always remind you of these things, even though you know them and are firmly established in the truth you now have. ¹³I think it is right to refresh your memory as long as I

> *live in the tent of this body, [14]because I know that I will soon*
> *put it aside, as our Lord Jesus Christ has made clear to me.*
> *[15]And I will make every effort to see that after my departure*
> *you will always be able to remember these things.*

Even strong Christians benefit from being reminded of
the basics of the gospel. Surely you have noticed how often a
sermon intended primarily for outsiders, explaining repentance
and baptism, ends up encouraging the disciples the most! We
all need reminders. That's why we read the Scriptures daily, as
God instructs. That's also why we celebrate communion weekly,
as God has ordained.

Peter is soon to be executed. Jesus intimated the kind of
death by which he would glorify God in John 21:18-19. Hence
he's all the more zealous to safeguard the church. The accepted
date of his crucifixion was 64 A.D., so this letter must have
been produced in 63 or 64 A.D., the tenth or eleventh year of
Nero's reign. But this was not Peter's first time on "death row."
(See Acts 12.)

Now what kind of a man would execute a servant and
apostle of Jesus Christ? Someone with little conscience, someone with a cruel streak as wide as the Amazon—someone like
Nero. Nero was one of the most morally deficient of all the
emperors known to mankind:

> He had received the finest of pagan philosophical educations, and yet
> he degenerated into one of the worst conceivable men. He visited broth-
> els, frequently in disguise. He practiced, as one historian says, "lewd-
> ness on boys...striking, wounding, murdering." He took a mistress. He
> wanted to have an affair with her, and his wife objected. What do you
> do in a case like that? Well, it should be obvious to any and all: you
> simply kill your wife!—which is what he did. But his mother objected.
> So he killed his mother...[1]

And so he married his mistress. Then one day she made the
sad mistake of nagging him because he came home late from
the races. She was in the latter stages of pregnancy. Nero kicked
her in the stomach, killing both her and the child. Keep in
mind, this was the ruler of the world at that time! It was indeed a cruel age.

---

[1] D. J. Kennedy, *What If Jesus Had Never Been Born?* (Nashville: Thomas Nelson), pp.
206-207.

Because of a man like this, Peter was soon to depart this world, but he was eager to ensure that the disciples not lose the thread of pure Christianity.

? What are the aspects of your faith in Jesus about which you need frequent reminders? Who is in your life to remind you? Do you thank them?

> *[16]We did not follow cleverly invented stories when we told you about the power and coming of our Lord Jesus Christ, but we were eyewitnesses of his majesty. [17]For he received honor and glory from God the Father when the voice came to him from the Majestic Glory, saying, "This is my Son, whom I love; with him I am well pleased." [18]We ourselves heard this voice that came from heaven when we were with him on the sacred mountain.*

"Cleverly invented stories" (literally "myths,") are *not* the substance of real Christianity. It is often asserted or implied that ancient peoples and Christians in particular were too naive to be able to distinguish truth from myth. This is pure hogwash!

The disciples were in shock when Jesus walked on water (whether or not they understood the principles of surface tension or fluid mechanics), and they were also in shock when he walked into a locked room without the benefit of a key! Joseph may not have had our modern scientific understanding, but he knew enough biology to realize the enigma of Mary's pregnancy—which is why he had in mind to divorce her. Peter himself knew the difference between fact and fiction and was willing to *die* for the historical truth he was convinced of.

Other religions (such as Hinduism, animism and Greco-Roman religion) rely heavily on myth; Christianity loudly proclaims that if this is myth, we should throw in the towel (1 Corinthians 15:19, 32).

The reference to the Transfiguration requires some explanation. Why would Peter choose that event to support his claim to be a faithful eyewitness? Surely there were other, more impressive miracles in which Jesus was involved? (At least it's something I've wondered about.)

To begin with, this is one of the events which only three men witnessed, and Peter, perhaps at this moment more than any other he shared in the presence of Jesus, was keenly aware of the majesty and transcendence of Christ. He wants us as disciples never to lose that reverence. At any rate, Peter's recollection of the event, the situation and the exact words is powerful evidence that he is a credible witness, that the faith is anchored firmly in history.

On the mountain of transfiguration Jesus met with Moses and Elijah to discuss his death—the death of the single individual who is the focal point of history! Moses represented the Law, Elijah the prophets (together they represented the Old Law), while Jesus represented the gospel. "Listen to him" means that, though Jesus' message doesn't do away with the Old Law, he is the one you must heed in order to understand its purpose and its fulfillment. "You will do well to pay attention to it" in verse 19 points back to the Transfiguration incident. Truly, the life and teachings of Jesus Christ in the New Testament are the key to grasping the Old Testament.

As someone has put it, "The Old Testament is the New Testament concealed; the New Testament is the Old Testament revealed." Are you striving for a mastery of the Old Testament? Are you imagining how our early brothers and sisters presented the gospel—with only the Old Testament to work from?

> [19]*And we have the word of the prophets made more certain, and you will do well to pay attention to it, as to a light shining in a dark place, until the day dawns and the morning star rises in your hearts.* [20]*Above all, you must understand that no prophecy of Scripture came about by the prophet's own interpretation.* [21]*For prophecy never had its origin in the will of man, but men spoke from God as they were carried along by the Holy Spirit.*

"We have the word of the prophets made more certain" (1:19) because Jesus has fulfilled the prophets and revealed the ultimate conclusion of their message.

The rising of the morning star in our hearts (1:19) has been interpreted variously as: a reference to the second coming of Christ (perhaps), to the enlightenment we receive when a passage of scripture becomes clear (too airy-fairy for me!), or as an allusion to Isaiah 8:20 (which is quite possible). Simon Pe-

ter is preparing to lambaste the false prophets—see 2 Peter 2—
and this little paragraph nicely bridges his thoughts on the
truth of the gospel with the *un*truth of the false prophets soon
to infect the Christian church.

If we fail to pay attention, we will drift into error. This is
Peter's worst fear. It compelled him to write his last letter.

On "Interpretation"

At this point three comments are in order concerning 2
Peter 1:19-21, since this section is widely used to argue both
for the inspiration of the whole Bible, and against the "private
interpretation" of Scripture.

- Strictly speaking, these verses apply only to the *prophetic*
parts of the Bible. By extension we might apply it to all of
Scripture (which happens to be true!), but that is taking
the verse out of context. Read the verse slowly and you'll
see what Peter had in mind.
- The "interpretation" Peter is talking about isn't the reader's
interpretation, but the inspired prophet's. Now you might
reason, "If the prophet wasn't at liberty to filter the will of
God, who are we to 'interpret' the Word to suit our
convenience?" Good! This is a legitimate inference, though
it's not what Peter had in mind. All Peter is saying is that
the true prophets accurately revealed the will of God—which
is far from what the false prophets were doing.
- Finally, we all "interpret" the Bible. To interpret means
simply to attempt to comprehend, to translate into
meaningful terms. No one reads the Bible without
interpretation. Interpretation is good. We should not tell
people we don't interpret it—that's nonsense. If we don't
interpret, then we don't understand. What you mean is
that you don't interpret it to suit your own convenience or
preconceptions; that is, you don't *twist* it.

Summary

In short, Peter urged his readers to concentrate. Remember
the words of Jesus Christ and the events of his life; distinguish
them from the cleverly invented stories of the false prophets

and teachers; and understand that real inspiration is from God, not from man. Do these things and you will avoid falling into the trap of the devil; you will never fall! That is certain, because *light overcomes darkness.*

Peter has now laid the foundation for his powerful appeal in the epistle of 2 Peter. In the next chapter he will really go for the jugular, warning the saints against the slavery awaiting them should they be sucked back into the world.

? How often do you reread the gospel accounts of Jesus' life? How much conviction about Jesus do others see in your eyes and hear in your voice?

15

Slavery and Suction
2 PETER 2

S econd Peter 2 is one of the most hard-hitting chapters in the New Testament. In it the apostle exposes the moral depravity of the false teachers who were to plague the Christian church for countless centuries. With their twisted gospels and their twisted lives, they would suck the life out of the church of Christ.

> *¹But there were also false prophets among the people, just as there will be false teachers among you. They will secretly introduce destructive heresies, even denying the sovereign Lord who bought them—bringing swift destruction on themselves. ²Many will follow their shameful ways and will bring the way of truth into disrepute. ³In their greed these teachers will exploit you with stories they have made up. Their condemnation has long been hanging over them, and their destruction has not been sleeping.*

In light of all that has happened to Christianity in the past two millennia, it is not surprising that the apostle prepared us in advance. Verses 1-3 provide a concise overview of the pattern of false doctrines and practices of the increasingly apostate church.

Peter prophesied a parallel between Israelite apostasy and "Christian" apostasy. Remember, the ratio of true prophets to false in OT times was often as poor as 1:100. In NT times it hardly seems better. When asked point-blank whether only a few were to be saved (Luke 13:24), Jesus wisely refused to give the percentage. Instead he charged the questioner to make every effort (*agonidzesthe*, "agonize") to enter through the narrow door. The point is not to know how many will be saved, but to be ready!

Following is a sampling of false doctrines and practices propagated through the centuries. These were spread through wishful thinking, careless exegesis, the non-inspired guesses of church leaders and much philosophical double-talk.

Altars	Apocrypha	Apparitions
Celibate clergy	Clergy-laity	Confessional
Confirmation	Crusades	"Faith alone"
Female pastors	Fusion of church/state	"Glossolalia"
Holy days	Holy laughter	Homosexual clergy
Indulgences	Infant baptism	Icons and statues
Inquisition	Liberation theology	Mary queen of heaven
"Millennial" kingdom	Monks and nuns	New Age Movement
NT Sabbath	Once saved always saved	Papacy
Prayers for dead	Prayers to saints	"Predestination"
Priesthood	Purgatory	Segregated services
Simony	"Slaying in the Spirit"	Transubstantiation
	Praying Jesus into your heart	

Teachers of such things deny the Lord—just as Peter did three times on a cold night nearly 20 centuries ago. Most false doctrines do the same: they deny or water down the Lordship of Christ. Repentance, commitment and a disciple's heart—without these essentials of a Christlike life, there can be no living hope.

And what's the motive behind false teachings? Greed. Human exploitation. Not that religious exploiters are more common than secular ones. (Most exploitation is committed by the irreligious.) It's just that it's less excusable in those who claim to follow Jesus.

Take a good look at the denominations. Do you see financial scandal? Yes, in abundance. What is the lifestyle of the highest echelon leaders in the denominations? Opulence? Sadly, this is often the case. Instead of feeding the flock, these leaders are fleecing it. Are unscrupulous men of wealth and power freely allowed to frequent the fellowship? In one large denomination, there is little sense of family—but then there is *the* family! (Ever heard of Mafiosi being disfellowshipped? It's doubtful you ever will. There are reasons for this; don't be naive.)

Church group after church group is rocked by financial and sexual scandal. Sin is winked at, condoned, tolerated. False teachers whitewash the sin and lukewarmness (Ezekiel 13) and false prophets dress the grievous wounds of the people lightly (Jeremiah 6). There are so many pseudo-Christian churches because of sin, selfishness and greed. God assures us they will most emphatically *not* get away with it in the end.

> *⁴For if God did not spare angels when they sinned, but sent them to hell, putting them into gloomy dungeons to be held for judgment; ⁵if he did not spare the ancient world when he brought the flood on its ungodly people, but protected Noah, a preacher of righteousness, and seven others; ⁶if he condemned the cities of Sodom and Gomorrah by burning them to ashes, and made them an example of what is going to happen to the ungodly; ⁷and if he rescued Lot, a righteous man, who was distressed by the filthy lives of lawless men ⁸(for that righteous man, living among them day after day, was tormented in his righteous soul by the lawless deeds he saw and heard)—⁹if this is so, then the Lord knows how to rescue godly men from trials and to hold the unrighteous for the day of judgment, while continuing their punishment. ¹⁰This is especially true of those who follow the corrupt desire of the sinful nature and despise authority.*
>
> *Bold and arrogant, these men are not afraid to slander celestial beings; ¹¹yet even angels, although they are stronger and more powerful, do not bring slanderous accusations against such beings in the presence of the Lord.*

God has not even spared angels punishment, nor a host of evil persons throughout history, so there is no need to fret: all flesh will be humbled, the evildoers will not prosper and every knee will bow. (Take a look at Psalm 73, which contains OT reflections on this theme with assurances that God's way will prevail in the end.)

? When is the last time you challenged a "bold and arrogant" person? Why must it be done? How can you do that without being bold and arrogant yourself?

Digression: Fun Facts About Angels

Angels are the subject of increasing interest and speculation these days. Here are some biblical facts for your consideration. Some of them may surprise you.

- The Greek word *angelos* means the same as the Hebrew word *malak:* "messenger or angel." They are subordinate beings, God's errand-boys.
- There are various orders of angelic beings: cherubim (Genesis 3:24) and seraphim (Isaiah 6:2); angels, authorities, powers (1 Peter 3:22; Colossians 2:15); archangels, possibly only one (besides Satan) (1 Thessalonians 4:16); thrones, powers, rulers and authorities (Colossians 1:16); celestial beings (2 Peter 2:10); ordinary angels and possibly others (Ephesians 6:12). The Bible provides no developed angelology, and it is possible that some of these terms overlap or are synonymous. At the theater we focus on the principal and minor characters on stage, not on the "messengers" like stage hands, technicians, make-up artists, and the host of others who are important but nonetheless unseen. Their work is evident, but they themselves are behind the scenes and out of sight. So it is with angels.
- Angels do not marry and they may well be sexless (Matthew 22:30). This seems enough to refute the prevalent idea that angels and human females brought forth a mutant race upon the earth (based on a dubious and superstitious interpretation of Genesis 6).
- Like humans and unlike God, they are bound in the world of space-time (Daniel 10:13).
- They are virtually never recognizable (Judges 13:21). They took many different forms in the Bible. Beware claims of people seeing angels; this is a highly improbable or at best, a rare event. Hebrews 13:2, in the context of hospitality, seems to refer to Abraham (Genesis 18-19) not to your chance to personally entertain an angel!
- The Bible does seem to support the traditional notion of guardian angels (Matthew 18:10; Acts 12:15).
- Jesus never appeared as an angel (Hebrews 9:26-28).
- Satan is probably a fallen archangel. (Luke 10:18 may refer to the fall of Satan in his rebellion against God, but more likely it refers to the retreat of Satan and his powers before the advancing forces of the gospel.)
- Some angels are "elect," others are damned and there seems to be no provision for the salvation of the damned ones (1 Timothy 5:21). Any reconciliation, whether ongoing or that may have occurred in the past, came through Christ (Colossians 1:20).

- Angels are described as "flying" but they're never described as having wings (Daniel 9:21).
- We don't become angels when we die, only like them in some respects (Matthew 22:30). (*The Littlest Angel* and other stories have popularized this misconception.)
- They serve the disciples (Hebrews 1:14). That means you are important and moreso than angels, so do not worship them—Colossians 2:18!)

? Although all your questions about angels are probably not answered, what about angels is most encouraging to your life?

A natural question arising from 2 Peter 2:4-11 is: What happens between death and judgment day for humans? (We already know what happens to wicked angels because Peter has just told us.) The phrase (actually one word) rendered "sent them to hell" is the Greek "sent or put them in Tartaros," which is "the abode of the dead" in Greek mythology. "Tartaros" to the Greeks was a place of darkness, gloom and unhappiness: the inevitable fate of mortals. Now, use of a word familiar from mythology in no way indicates serious credence in myths. (We use words like Wednesday, Thursday, Friday and Saturday without being accused of superstitious belief in the Nordic gods *Woden, Thor, Freja,* or the Roman *Saturnus.*) Peter's readers knew (better than we do) what God was communicating.

Verse 9 tells us that after death the unrighteous are punished—even before the Judgment Day. In my view Luke 16:19-31, though a parable, shows reward and punishment *before* the judgment. Neither the full reward nor the full punishment, but an opportunity to savor what is to come (for the saints) and to dread the just sentence with sober reflection (for the lost). We must be careful, however, about drawing theological conclusions from parables and isolated, relatively obscure passages of scripture![1]

Noah was a "preacher" or "herald" of righteousness. This is the same word used of Jesus in 1 Peter 3:19 (see Chapter 10). Sodom and Gomorrah were incinerated; Peter says this is an example of what will happen to the ungodly in the destroying (2 Peter 2:12) fire of hell. Lot was rescued, and with Noah,

[1] Technical point: the NIV alternate translation found in the footnote, softens this teaching by translating *koladzomenous* "for punishment" instead of by the straightforward participial phrase, the consensus view of the translators, attempts to avoid difficulties arising in punishment being meted out *before* the official verdict is read.)

serves as an example of a faithful person being rescued from trial. This was immediately relevant to the Christians of Peter's day. They needed that encouragement. (And so do we!)

New Testament Insights into Old Testament Hearts

Sometimes items in the OT are unintelligible without the NT and vice versa. In this chapter, three heart insights come to light, none of which is clear in the OT.

The first insight concerns Noah: he preached. That is never explicitly stated in the text of Genesis, though it is hard to think he would not have said a thing or two during the century it took him to build the ark, isn't it?

The second insight: Lot was tormented in his soul. From Genesis you would think he was at times nothing more than a "careless compromiser," a spineless, drunken character not fit to figure positively in the pages of the holy writ. But Peter insists he was righteous, despite his sin and weakness.

Third: Balaam son of Beor (mentioned below), hired by the Moabite king to curse Israel (Numbers 22-25;31:8; Deuteronomy 23:4-5), loved money. You suspect he struggled with materialism, but it's only in 2 Peter that God explicitly reveals that he loved the wages of wickedness. Once again, we see that "The New Testament is the Old Testament revealed."

[12]But these men blaspheme in matters they do not understand. They are like brute beasts, creatures of instinct, born only to be caught and destroyed, and like beasts they too will perish.

[13]They will be paid back with harm for the harm they have done. Their idea of pleasure is to carouse in broad daylight. They are blots and blemishes, reveling in their pleasures while they feast with you. [14]With eyes full of adultery, they never stop sinning; they seduce the unstable; they are experts in greed—an accursed brood! [15]They have left the straight way and wandered off to follow the way of Balaam son of Beor, who loved the wages of wickedness. [16]But he was rebuked for his wrongdoing by a donkey—a beast without speech—who spoke with a man's voice and restrained the prophet's madness.

[17]These men are springs without water and mists driven by a storm. Blackest darkness is reserved for them. [18]For they mouth empty, boastful words and, by appealing to the lustful

desires of sinful human nature, they entice people who are
just escaping from those who live in error.

Why is Peter so scathing in his denunciation of the false
prophets? God takes rebellion, arrogance, perversion and god-
lessness seriously. Why? *Because they destroy life.* The traits
mentioned above are especially prevalent in the wave of "lib-
erated" morals and values that have taken the Western world
by storm, especially since the 1960s. Yes, freedom was promised, but what did we get? Broken dreams, broken promises,
broken families and broken hearts; renewed outbreaks of sexual
disease; increased corruption and welfare fraud; softness in
personal discipline and in the work ethic, coupled with mis-
leading "positive thinking" books which remove emphasis
from hard work to naive, dreamy reverie; breakdown of the
family and a whole new generation of unruly children and
teens, reared under the unwise tutelage of Dr. Spock; violence
in schools and declining standards of education; a prevailing
feeling of meaninglessness that has led philosophers, artists
and many others to suicide—need I go on?

Peter insists that the most obvious fruit of a godless world-
view is *sexual sin.* Expect it to be rampant in societies, and
even churches, where truth is routinely compromised and the
gospel soft-peddled.

We are different from the animals, despite the protests of
the ultra-green. When we forget this truth, we suffer moral
declension; we start behaving like animals. Far from being
"natural" and good, this is unnatural, pathetic and tragic.

"Feast" (2:13) in this passage is probably a reference to the
original Christian practice of the communion meal.

The observant reader will notice a number of similarities
between 2 Peter 2-3 and Jude. Many scholars believe that Jude
(Jesus' brother—Matthew 13:55) has borrowed from Peter. Biblical writers frequently borrow from one another, and this is
no hindrance to belief in the inspiration of Jude. On the other
hand, Peter may have gotten his inspiration from Jude then
expanded on it. (That *is* in the nature of preachers!)

"Eyes full of adultery" (2:14) is an allusion to Jesus' words
in the Sermon on the Mount (Matthew 5:28). Remember, *Peter
was an eyewitness!* You'd think these men would really stand

out—they are described in such lurid terms! They *do* stand out, but because of our own softness we may fail to notice them. How is *your* conviction?

The "straight way" is the narrow road of Matthew 7:14. The fact that these brutish men had *left* the straight and narrow shows they had *fallen away.* When someone falls away, he not only falls away from the fellowship, but from his "first love" (Revelation 2:4-5) and from the high moral standards of Christ. It is an abysmal fall indeed!

> [19]*They promise them freedom, while they themselves are slaves of depravity—for a man is a slave to whatever has mastered him.* [20]*If they have escaped the corruption of the world by knowing our Lord and Savior Jesus Christ and are again entangled in it and overcome, they are worse off at the end than they were at the beginning.* [21]*It would have been better for them not to have known the way of righteousness, than to have known it and then to turn their backs on the sacred command that was passed on to them.* [22]*Of them the proverbs are true: "A dog returns to its vomit," and, "A sow that is washed goes back to her wallowing in the mud."*

These people have *escaped* the corruption of the world by knowledge of Christ. Reread 2 Peter 1:3-4. They were truly saved, then once again truly lost. For all its popularity, the doctrine of "once saved, always saved" is misguided, demotivating, and malignant. It *is* possible to fall away, and it is cheap reasoning to insist that anyone who appeared to be a Christian and then quit was never really saved in the first place. Peter thinks otherwise. In fact he says it would be better if they had never become Christians! A helpful passage, Luke 12:47-48, explains why. The severest punishment in hell is that reserved for those who know the truth and then fall away. Then Peter compares these turncoats to "dogs" and "pigs." (The adage about the dog comes from one of the "fool" cycles, in Proverbs 26:3-12.) How *fool*ish to fall away! Once again, the influence of the Sermon on the Mount is evident. Jesus is unbelievably blunt. Matthew 7:6 says your spiritual energies are wasted on dogs and pigs. They don't appreciate your "pearls," nor do they have a taste for spiritual things. They might even turn on you and attack!

These godless people are marked by slavery and suction. They want *you*. Peter has much more to say about the coming godless generation in 2 Peter 3!

? How does our world promise freedom? How does it fail to deliver? To which lie of the world are you most susceptible? What action do you take to resist the false claims?

16

Water and Fire
2 PETER 3

"S ome say the world will end by fire, some say by ice...." So goes the well-known poem. Of course, exactly how it will end is immaterial (no pun intended); the point is to be ready. The false prophets have got it all wrong. If they are right, there is nothing you need to do to get ready; if they are wrong, they are influencing millions to make the worst spiritual and cosmic blunder they could possibly make.

The stakes are high. True knowledge of God is what will pull us through. Pay close attention to Peter's final chapter in his "memoirs."

> *¹Dear friends, this is now my second letter to you. I have written both of them as reminders to stimulate you to wholesome thinking. ²I want you to recall the words spoken in the past by the holy prophets and the command given by our Lord and Savior through your apostles.*

Notice that Peter states this is his second letter. Now the first is almost certainly 1 Peter, assuming 2 Peter was sent to the same regions named in 1 Peter 1:1. This may seem obvious, yet consider Paul's letters: he mentions a previous letter to the Corinthians (2 Corinthians 7:8) which, from context, cannot be 1 Corinthians. (Paul even mentions a letter before 1 Corinthians in 1 Corinthians 5:9!) When reading a passage in an epistle, one question that must be asked is: To whom is the author writing?

Notice also how Peter speaks of himself in the third person (3:2). In the ancient world this was common practice, and should in no way be interpreted as meaning the author was not Peter, as liberal theologians and clergymen hold. For a parallel, see Ephesians 2:20 and 3:5. This practice of the author referring to himself in the third person may be modesty; more likely it was simply the convention of the day.

> *³First of all, you must understand that in the last days scoffers will come, scoffing and following their own evil desires. ⁴They will say, "Where is this 'coming' he promised? Ever since our fathers died, everything goes on as it has since the beginning of creation." ⁵But they deliberately forget that long ago by God's word the heavens existed and the earth was formed out of water and by water. ⁶By these waters also the world of that time was deluged and destroyed.*

"Scoffers" (2:3) will come. For more on the character of these people, read the "mocker" passages in the book of Proverbs. Don't suppose they were not religious men: The opponents of the truth in 2 Peter create spiritual concoctions (2:3), partake of the communion (2:13) and in the past had been converted (2:21).

Not surprisingly, false teachers make light of the Judgment Day. It is in their own selfish interest to contradict the high moral requirements of God and the coming day of accountability. People who have problems with accountability detest the notion of the Judgment—even though they may give lip service to the idea.

The argument from history that "life goes on" is a very poor one. All agree that human life began at some point, and most agree that there must be an *end* as well, sooner or later. Time and history are *linear*, not *circular*. The gaping hole in the scoffers' logic is "deliberate" (3:5). They were cocksure nothing shocking would happen—how convenient! Also not surprisingly, though the collective memory of human culture overflows with the memory of the Flood, scoffers minimize or deny the account of Noah and the Deluge. They have no fear of God.

> *⁷By the same word the present heavens and earth are reserved for fire, being kept for the day of judgment and destruction of ungodly men.*

The ungodly will be destroyed by fire. God will completely eliminate them from the universe. The fire of hell is a biblical teaching. Peter doesn't hesitate to refer to it when he needs to, nor should we, despite the fact that the overwhelming thrust of the gospel is good news.

> [8]*But do not forget this one thing, dear friends: With the Lord a day is like a thousand years, and a thousand years are like a day.* [9]*The Lord is not slow in keeping his promise, as some understand slowness. He is patient with you, not wanting anyone to perish, but everyone to come to repentance.*

With God "a day is like a thousand years" (2:8). This is opposite the point Moses makes in Psalm 90:4. In 2 Peter the *slowness* of passage of time with God is stressed. This is to man's benefit. In Psalm 90 Moses stresses the *swiftness* of the passage of time with man: a thousand years fly past like a day or a watch in the night (four hours). Life is short.[1]

The slowness of Christ's return is not for our convenience, but so that more people will repent! God expects us to repent. As in Romans 2, God's kindness is an incentive and an opportunity for us to repent. We serve a good God. This is important because if, deep down in our hearts, we suspect that the Being who steers the universe is unfair, arbitrary, sadistic, evil or a monster, every area of our Christian life will be skewed. Imagine if, in our hearts, we feared that God was not so good after all. Take our evangelism: How could we eagerly invite others to bind themselves to an angry, malevolent power? We couldn't. We would believe in our hearts that we were annoying the non-Christians, even doing them a disservice! Take prayer: How could we keep our fervor to pray to this exploiter of mankind or being whose "love" for us is feigned? We wouldn't! And so it is with those who don't trust that God is good.

> [10]*But the day of the Lord will come like a thief. The heavens will disappear with a roar; the elements will be destroyed by fire, and the earth and everything in it will be laid bare.* [11]*Since everything will be destroyed in this way, what kind*

---

[1]Those who take the six days of Genesis as six thousand-year periods find no support for their theory here. To play their game, 1000 years = 1 day, *or* 1000 years = 1/6 of a day (a Hebrew watch, not the Roman 3-hour watch). So is a "day" 1000 years, or 6000 years? (36,000 years of creation?) The Mormons have actually calculated a celestial "minute"! Enough of this!

*of people ought you to be? You ought to live holy and godly
lives* [12]*as you look forward to the day of God and speed its
coming. That day will bring about the destruction of the heav-
ens by fire, and the elements will melt in the heat.*

The day comes like a thief, not so that we'll be caught off
guard, but because if we knew the exact time, our motives
would be wrong. God wants our response to his patience to be
genuine, spontaneous and purely motivated.

Everything will burn (2:10): There are, in fact, only three
things that will survive the fire: God, the word of God and the
people of God. Everything material will dissolve. Peter even
says that God will use this fire for the punishment and destruction of ungodly men (3:7).

"Speed its coming" (3:12)? How can we do that? Should
we prefer the translations which read "wait eagerly for..."? The
Greek *speudontas* ("hasten; hurry; exert oneself; be zealous
[for]") normally means "hasten." So, yes, we can, by the way
that we live, accelerate the return of Jesus to the earth. What a
thought!

? How does it affect you to know that so many of things people work so hard for in
this world will all be destroyed by fire? In view of this end, what is really important?

The End of the World

Many individuals and groups have claimed to know the
date of the end of the world, the day of Christ's coming again
to the earth. This is an issue of tremendous interest among the
denominations, who should take the warning of Amos more
soberly:

> *Woe to you who long for the day of the Lord!*
> *Why do you long for the day of the Lord?...*
> *Will not the day of the Lord be darkness, not light—*
>   *pitch-dark, without a ray of brightness?*
>
> *"I hate, I despise your religious feasts;*
>   *I cannot stand your assemblies"* (Amos 5:18, 20-21).

Amos, in the eighth century B.C., prophesied about the
"end" of Israel: her punishment through the dreaded Assyrians.

They were sure that in their own righteousness they had nothing to fear. But God hated then (as now) their lukewarm, hypocritical religion, which will do nothing to save them on the day of darkness. In the same way, God has forewarned all men of the Judgment Day, of the punishment to come not just on one nation, but on the entire world—and he has commanded them to repent, to be ready (Acts 17:30).

What facts can we know for sure concerning the end? Though this is a stunningly broad and commented-upon field, here are a few facts we can know with certainty concerning the end:

Facts About the End

- The bottom line: *No one knows* when the end will come (1 Thessalonians 5:2). Hence it follows that anyone who claims to know is a deceiver. Every generation of Christians has lived in hope of the coming of Christ, as far as church history reads. Countless due dates have come and gone; many otherwise brilliant minds have been deceived into risking reputation and sometimes fortune for the whims of human speculation. The smart thing is not to play the (guessing) game.
- So have nothing to do with those groups which play with prophecies and arrogantly trumpet their insight into the "end-times." Most notable among the false prophets are the Jehovah's Witnesses, who have continually predicted the end of the world: 1914, 1918, 1925, 1941,1975...
- All that counts is being right with God. Those fixated on the "Second Coming" seldom (ironically) spend much time helping the lost to be prepared! (By the way, "Second Coming" is a human term, not the Bible's. In fact, there are several "comings" of Jesus or God in the Bible—an interesting topic for future study! Ask a Christian whose knowledge you respect to point out some of them to you.
- Actually *no* chapter of the Bible provides "signs" of the end. Matthew 24, often cited as an "end-times" passage, prophesies the destruction of Jerusalem by the Romans in 70 A.D. Everything written in Matthew 24:1-33 was fulfilled in *that* generation (according to v. 34)—or Jesus was in error! An understanding of the OT background of the text and terms overwhelmingly supports this view.

- The same could be said of Revelation, which the author explicitly says would *soon* be fulfilled (Revelation 1:1, 1:3). This book of prophecy applies directly to the Roman Empire, persecutions she was dealing out to the disciples, and punishment which would swiftly fall on her at the hand of God. Once again, it is easier to get the most out of such passages when you have had a grounding in OT history and literature.
- There will not be two resurrections, as many maintain. John 5:25, 28-29 shows clearly that all will be resurrected simultaneously.
- Many believers take the seven days of Genesis as the framework for human history: 4,000 years before Christ, 2,000 years during the "church age," and afterwards a millennium ("1,000 years," Latin) of peace on earth as the Messiah reigns from Jerusalem. All this hinges on a dubious use of Psalm 90:4 and an unwarranted literalization of Revelation 20:2. In actuality when the Lord returns, the earth will be destroyed—all on the same "day." The literalists, with their comic (not cosmic) speculations, have it wrong!
- The Christian bookstores are filled with speculative and unbiblical reading about the end times. Is it just coincidence that there is big money in playing on people's curiosity and fear concerning this subject?

Incidentally, most fundamentalists insist Jesus will return in our lifetime. The term "fundamentalist" actually has a very specific meaning of which few Christians are adequately aware. In 1910-1912 the twelve-volume *The Fundamentals,* released by conservative scholars, taught many things, such as the virgin birth, the physical resurrection of Christ, the literal interpretation of the Bible (notoriously difficult to enforce!) as well as the imminent, physical second coming. Those who subscribed to these beliefs were called "fundamentalists." However, it must be stressed that not all Bible-believers believe Jesus will return in our generation.

- Jesus *may* come in our lifetime, yet we should be cautious in assuming we can second-guess God or force his hand. What about "speeding his coming" (2 Peter 3:12)—does our evangelism hasten the end? Apparently so, but the definition of an "evangelized world" is open to discussion. This is *not* to say we should not in faith make every effort to evangelize the world. In short, there could be a lag between the "final" person who is baptized and the return of our Lord. God is sovereign, and he will decide.

> [13]*But in keeping with his promise we are looking forward to a new heaven and a new earth, the home of righteousness.*

The "new heaven and a new earth" are not literal. Isaiah 65:17 is the source of the concept, where the phrase describes a new state of affairs, a new beginning, a fresh start. Jehovah's Witnesses and other groups teach the doctrine of a rejuvenated planet, completely missing the reference to the Isaiah passage and its metaphorical fulfillment in the return of the Jewish people from captivity.

? What are some things in this world to which you are looking forward? How do these things compare with "the home of righteousness"?

> [14]*So then, dear friends, since you are looking forward to this, make every effort to be found spotless, blameless and at peace with him.*

Since everything will burn, *all physical things are relativized.* It's not that the physical realm is intrinsically evil or that disciples should neglect it, but it's just not worth the high price tag Satan has put on it. In *his* world all that really counts (truth, souls, virtue, relationships, dignity) is cheapened, and all that is cheap or worldly is glorified, worshipped and grossly magnified: money, pleasure, material comfort, fame, fashion, acceptance, career, education and more. Peter puts everything in perspective: Everything's going to burn; get a grip; hold to what is truly valuable.

> [15]*Bear in mind that our Lord's patience means salvation, just as our dear brother Paul also wrote you with the wisdom that God gave him.* [16]*He writes the same way in all his letters, speaking in them of these matters. His letters contain some things that are hard to understand, which ignorant and unstable people distort, as they do the other Scriptures, to their own destruction.*

The Lord's patience means salvation. Peter's reference to Paul's letters is most likely to Romans 2:4-9. Some of Paul's writings (which Peter says are inspired, 3:16) contain difficult bits. Not impossible bits, but ones which the reader must pore over and come to grips with. Paul himself, in his second letter to the Corinthians, insists that it isn't his way to speak over people's heads, to deliberately confuse, to obfuscate (2 Corinthians 1:13).

What is the consequence of twisting the Scriptures? Destruction. And who perverts the Scriptures? Ignorant and unstable people. So the difficulty of the Bible is not the reason false doctrine is generated; it is the ignorance and instability (morally and spiritually) of the false teachers.

> [17]*Therefore, dear friends, since you already know this, be on your guard so that you may not be carried away by the error of lawless men and fall from your secure position.* [18]*But grow in the grace and knowledge of our Lord and Savior Jesus Christ. To him be glory both now and forever! Amen.*

As disciples of Christ we do enjoy a secure position. Where in this world do we find real security? Relationships often leave us "high and dry." Financial security comes and goes, for wealth is so uncertain (1 Timothy 6:17). Job security for many is less secure now than ever. But in Christ we have a firm foundation from which we can never be moved, providing we keep our eyes open (1 Peter 5:8)!

Peter urges us to be on our guard. As Christians in one sense we can breathe, relax and be free from anxiety. In another sense we can *never* let up, not even for a minute. Every sin, every moment of slackness, every careless thought, word or deed will be used by Satan to further *his* kingdom.

And yet, like God, Satan works primarily through the agency of individual people. That's why Peter warns us not to be carried away by the error of lawless men (lawless in that they selfishly insist on their *own* law or way, not God's law).

If we are carried away by these false teachers, we *can* fall from our secure position. The error of those who do not know God's law operates in several ways:

• false doctrines
• diluted gospel preaching

- hypocritical clergymen
- illegitimate denominations
- false promises of "freedom"
- challenges to spiritual authority

Like Paul, Peter knew full well that "the secret power of lawlessness is already at work" (2 Thessalonians 2:7). "Sin is lawlessness" (1 John 3:4), John reminds us. Lawlessness is "doing what is right in our *own* eyes," as in the days of the Judges (Judges 21:25). This spirit of lawlessness is powerfully at work in our world and among the multitude of denominations that purport to be Christian.

"Fall" (3:17) means "fall away," not "stumble"—in the way Psalm 37:24 illustrates. The alternative is to grow spiritually "in the grace and in the knowledge of Jesus Christ." Are you growing in knowledge? In grace? If not, your chances of falling are high.

So let us glorify him—not man, who is so easily derailed from the truth and pleased to worship his own spirit. Let's glorify him now, and let's also glorify him forever (in the eternal kingdom). Amen!

Summary

The time has come to wrap up the magnificent letter of 2 Peter. As we have seen, the theme is *the knowledge of God*. Peter ends the epistle with a warning, just as he ended 1 Peter (in 5:8). The great apostle truly had the spiritual welfare of the saints at heart!

This letter can change your life and ensure that you never fall—guaranteeing "the life to the full" God has planned for *you*. Consider for one last time the force and flow of 2 Peter:

Chapter 1: *Grace and growth* come only through the knowledge of God.
Chapter 2: *Twisted gospels and twisted lives* characterize the false teachers.
Chapter 3: *Fear God and further your knowledge of him,* and you'll never fall.

? What is your plan for continuing to grow in the grace and knowledge of Jesus Christ? What are some of the best ways to tell if you are growing? How much does it bother you if you find that growth is not happening in your life?

Part III

FROM DEATH TO LIFE

1-3 JOHN, JUDE

We know that we have passed from death to life, because we love our brothers. Anyone who does not love remains in death...This is how we know what love is: Jesus Christ laid down his life for us. And we ought to lay down our lives for our brothers.

1 JOHN 3:14, 16

Crossing over from death to life—our ultimate reward—is awesome. But Christians believe in more than this: We believe in life *before* death! These epistles of passion, penned by two of Jesus' most intimate friends, will encourage our souls. And such is the contrast between the worldly life and the spiritual life.

17

John and Jude: Straight Talk
INTRODUCTION

The apostle John and Jesus' brother Jude each give us a window into the heart of God. First there's John, the "beloved" apostle, who lay on Jesus' breast, probably the apostle closest to Jesus emotionally. Then there's Jude, one of Jesus' own family. John's style is simple, direct. Jude's is more colorful and sophisticated, but it has teeth. Each is concerned with the heresy that is creeping into the Christian church. Their horror and indignation is God's horror and indignation: at false teaching, at religious apathy and at blatant sin. They are God's mouthpiece. No mincing of words. No suggesting anything. Just straight talk.

The heresies of Gnosticism and Docetism (definitions to follow) plagued the church in the final third of the first century. In particular we need to examine the teachings of Gnosticism, a heresy which plagued the early church and even today is not entirely dead. The New Age Movement has numerous Gnostic elements masquerading as Christianity. It is winning a large following, particularly from among members of dead denominational churches.[1]

The Apostle John

John, like so many of Jesus' apostles, was a fisherman (Matthew 4:21). He was the brother of James (*not* the brother of

---

[1] There are several components to this movement, a modern day phenomenon that is sweeping away many people tired of traditional religion. New Age theology is a fusion of Eastern mysticism and Western concepts, with elements of astrology, pantheism, meditation, the occult and a good deal of snob appeal. In keeping with Eastern religion and philosophy, enlightenment is sought within, rather than without—at the foot of the cross of Christ. Therein lies the central flaw of this and many other quasi-religious movements. Sin is downplayed, and the language of love, unity and freedom masks the true heart of the movement, which throbs with rebellion and individualism. In the West the movement attempts to make orthodox Christianity palatable to all and takes strong exception to the doctrines of sin, judgment, righteousness, hell and other doctrines plainly set out in the Bible. The New Age message is seen clearly in such recent best sellers as *The Celestine Prophecy* and *The Care of the Soul*.

Jesus) and the son of Zebedee. Jesus nicknamed he and his
brother "Sons of Thunder." For his conviction? Resonating
voice? Harshness? (Luke 9:54). We can know that the epithet
has something to do with his character.

John was an elder (2 John 1; 3 John 1), thus married with
children who were believers. His writings are several: the Gospel of John, with its universal thrust and appeal; 1 John, which
confronts Gnosticism and Docetism; 2 John, which relates to
the same situation as 1 John; 3 John, which attempts to solve
an acute leadership crisis; and Revelation, a prophecy which
gave encouragement during the time of Roman oppression later
in the century.

There are multiple traditions about John's death. One says
that he alone escaped martyrdom and lived into his 90s or
100s, perhaps surviving into the second century. Another says
he was boiled in oil, yet emerged unscathed. But traditions are
traditions, not the word of God. John may have died early in
the reign of Domitian, or even under Vespasian or Titus. But
regardless, his influence outlasts him by thousands of years!

Jude

Jude was one of the four natural sons of Joseph and Mary
(Mark 6:3) and a brother of Jesus. Imagine having Jesus as your
eldest sibling! Interestingly, Jude does not dare to call himself
a brother of Jesus Christ (though that was half true) but rather
prefers the more humble title of servant (Jude 1:1). He also
reminds his readers that he is a (full) brother of James. Jude
and James must have been very well known for Jude to have
referred to himself and his brother so simply, and the case for
Jude being the Judas of Matthew 13:55 is quite strong.

Jude and James are the English names for *Ioudas* and *Iakobos,*
Greek for *Yehuda* and *Ya'aqov,* Hebrew for the famous patri-
arch and his father (Genesis). Incidentally, John and Peter come
from Greek names (no OT root), *Ioannes* ("Ee-oh-áh-nees") and
Petros.

Jude must have known Peter, and if you compare the short
letter of Jude with 2 Peter 2, you will see much common material. Scholars debate who has borrowed from whom (with per-
mission?), but the consensus is that Peter adapted Jude's material.

Gnosticism

The word "gnosticism" comes from *gnosis*, Greek for "knowledge." Here, esoteric or secret knowledge is meant with the Gnostics believing that only an elite few had a special enlightenment. The Gnostic view of matter had profound implications: Matter is evil. In their minds, true spirituality rose above the material world. Thus the god who made the material world (the god of the OT) is an inferior being. There are many gods, and many levels of spirituality. Gnosticism had two principal varieties: "ascetic" and "libertine." The ascetic strain advocated harsh treatment of the body, since flesh was evil. The libertine strain held that what you did to or with your body was irrelevant.

Docetism

Docetism is a corollary doctrine to Gnostic teaching. Because matter was inferior to spirit in their thinking, Jesus only *appeared* to have a body. The term comes from the Greek *dokein*, "seem." Had you followed Jesus around you would have found that he was a phantom figure who left no footprints! This is the heresy exposed in 1- and 2 John, where the apostle insists that Jesus came in a tangible and visible body (1 John 1:1, 4:2, 5:6). It was the deceivers who claimed that Jesus did not come in the flesh (2 John 7).

There are a number of NT references that begin making sense when you realize the nature of the false doctrine being discussed. Colossians 2:18-23 deals with ascetic regulations, and the specific heresy seems to be a fusion of Jewish and Gnostic philosophy. 1 Timothy 6:20 addresses the Gnostic superiority complex ("what is falsely called *knowledge*," emphasis added), while 1- and 2 John deal with Docetism. Jude seems to deal with a libertine form of gnosticism.

Philosophy and Theology

John's gospel shares a common thought world and speaks in the same ideological context as 1 John. In a masterful stroke, John turns Greek philosophy on its ear as he expounds the true nature of the *logos*. The opening paragraph of John's first epistle is strikingly similar to the opening of his gospel. The "word" (Greek, *logos*) in John 1 is equivalent to the "Word of Life" (*ho logos tes zoes*) in 1 John 1. Logos can mean "word, speech, declaration, matter, command, commission, message; account, reason, principle." For the Stoics *logos* referred to the divine principle that held the universe together. Several of these meanings may inhere in the description of Jesus as *logos*.

As disciples, we cannot say, "Philosophy and theology don't matter; just read the Bible." The fact is that words and ideas are powerful, and they influence hordes of unbelievers (and believers). We need to educate ourselves, whether about New Age teaching, Buddhism, Islam or existentialist philosophy. We have a moral obligation not only to teach the truth clearly, but also to protect the church from the ravages of false teachers. It *is* a matter of life and death. Just read the letters of John and Jude and see!

? Have you had any experiences with New Age teachings? Do you know anyone who attempts to combine some elements of Christianity with elements of Eastern religions, claiming that they are all very similar? What are some of the easiest ways to recognize that a teaching is false?

18

Light and Right
1 JOHN 1

In the last chapter we discussed the heresies of Gnosticism and Docetism which plagued the early church and are making a comeback through New Age teaching today. Now we're ready to begin our study of the Johannine epistles. 1 John is a letter from the apostle to Christians in Asia Minor (modern Turkey). These inspired words are addressed to the second generation of Christians. A whole generation of true disciples has been converted and died; it is up to their children to carry the torch.

> *¹That which was from the beginning, which we have heard, which we have seen with our eyes, which we have looked at and our hands have touched—this we proclaim concerning the Word of life. ²The life appeared; we have seen it and testify to it, and we proclaim to you the eternal life, which was with the Father and has appeared to us. ³We proclaim to you what we have seen and heard, so that you also may have fellowship with us. And our fellowship is with the Father and with his Son, Jesus Christ. ⁴We write this to make our joy complete.*

John is emphatic that Jesus Christ came in a *physical* body. His life and person were open to verification through the physical senses: sight, hearing and touch. (Remember, the Docetists are claiming that he came not in a physical body but as some sort of disembodied spirit.) As with nearly all the NT letters, 1 John is written to protect the church from error and guide it into the truth.

John insists he is a reliable eyewitness of Jesus Christ. It really does matter whether Jesus physically existed, whether he physically came to earth as a man, preached, loved and resisted temptation in the flesh, whether he physically died on a cross and physically rose from the dead! (Read through 1

Corinthians 15 if you're not quite sure how important all this is.) If we are living for a fairy tale—or for just one more nice religion—we are pitiful and pitiable!

John stresses here not the divinity of Jesus, but his humanity, which was being questioned. So, was Jesus 50% human and 50% divine? No! He was 100% human and 100% divine. Doesn't that add up to 200%? Yes, but it multiplies to 100%. As an illustration, a beverage may be totally wet and completely lime-green—100% of each—both at the same time non-miraculously. Neither quality excludes the other. In the same way Jesus is human and divine.

According to verse 2, eternal life—the quest of all mankind—is available to all through Jesus Christ. This means that none of us possesses it innately. Romans 6:23 tells us that eternal life is a *gift* we receive through Christ. This implies that no one will truly live eternally who has not come through Jesus Christ. And yet what an incredible gift for those willing to receive it!

Why the mention of "fellowship" in 1:3? Because the false teachers, influenced by the Gnostics, had left the fellowship. Either you are in the fellowship or out of it (in both senses of the phrase!). The Gnosticized Christians had "gone out" (1 John 2:19); their new "church" was not in fellowship with the real disciples—they had nothing in common.

> *5This is the message we have heard from him and declare to you: God is light; in him there is no darkness at all. 6If we claim to have fellowship with him yet walk in the darkness, we lie and do not live by the truth.*

Light and darkness don't mix, and woe to those who confuse the two! (Isaiah 5:20). Now is light perfection? No, light (John 3:19-21) is characteristic of God, his word and his people. In other words, judge these false Christians not just by their theology, but also by their morality. (Ephesians 5 is another chapter highlighting the darkness-light theme.)

? When is the last time you looked at a temptation and said, "No, I am not going to
• give in because that is darkness"? What things have you decided not to allow in your life because they belong to the darkness and not to the light?

*⁷But if we walk in the light, as he is in the light, we have fel-
lowship with one another, and the blood of Jesus, his Son,
purifies us from all sin. ⁸If we claim to be without sin, we de-
ceive ourselves and the truth is not in us. ⁹If we confess our
sins, he is faithful and just and will forgive us our sins and
purify us from all unrighteousness.*
    *¹⁰If we claim we have not sinned, we make him out to be a
liar and his word has no place in our lives.*

"Walking in the light"—is this possible for a mere human?
Absolutely Yes! The opponents of John's churches claimed to
be in the light, but they were not, for three reasons:

- They were not in fellowship with the true disciples. In fact
  they stood in opposition to the true disciples. (See 1 John
  4:5-6.)
- They did not walk in the light. They did not walk as disciples.
  (See 1 John 2:3-6.) Walking in the light does not mean
  perfection, but discipleship, as 2:6-7 makes clear. If it is
  impossible to walk in the light, then we are all lost, because
  walking as Jesus walked and walking in the light are one
  and the same.
- They did not admit to wrong and claimed to be without
  sin (1:8-10). "Walking in the light" is not only not
  perfection, it is a lifestyle where there is the open admission
  of imperfection. "Walking in the light" is parallel to
  "confessing our sins," that is, being open about our lives
  and refusing to hide what we are in the darkness (John
  3:19-21).

Do you enjoy walking in the light? Does guilt prevent you?
Some Christians falsely imagine that when they sin they go
back to the darkness, and when they confess they are forgiven
again and come back into the light. What agony! What insecu-
rity! What false doctrine! What a misunderstanding of grace,
a lapse into Galatians 3:3 theology!
    1 John 1:7-9 says that we are purified from sin even *while*
we are sinning, because (in our attitude) we are walking in the
light. Christians never go back and forth from darkness to light
unless they, leave the fellowship and at some later time are
restored. We have crossed from death to life; that's settled.
Once the bill is paid, we don't go back to the waitress and
"settle up" again! It's *paid*.

Confession is most important. It needs to be a part of our lifestyle. It is part of walking in the light. However, a Christian who fails to confess *every* sin is not going to be condemned. Imagine the scene at Judgment Day:

> *God:* "Smith, you almost made it. In fact you were one of the more faithful ones. But if you recall that day in August 1988, the 9th to be precise, you lapsed into laziness in the late afternoon, and you never confessed it!
>
> *Smith:* "Oh no, I thought I'd confessed everything! [Now sweating] What about my faith and all my deeds? All the church services? No! Not outer darkness!!!
>
> *God:* "I'm sorry, Smith, salvation depends on perfect confession. [To angels] Bind him and throw him on out!"
>
> *Smith:* "Aaaaaahhhh!"

It's sad that in their hearts many disciples fear this is God's way of dealing with people. They need to know the Savior—as he truly is, not as they imagine him!

Then how *are* Christians forgiven when they sin? Baptism and subsequent confession has been described as "a bath and a shower in the blood of Jesus." We as Christians don't need the bath again, but it sure feels good to shower off the unrighteousness in the presence of God. Granted, forgiveness is automatic, so why pray for forgiveness when our relationship with God is secure? Take marriage, for example. When we sin against our spouse, we need to ask for forgiveness. Forgiveness for what purpose? To become married again, or to mend the relationship? Christians ask for God's forgiveness *not* that they might be spared from going to hell (that was taken care of in the waters of baptism), but that the personal relationship with God might be healed. A son or daughter of God confesses sin not to be forgiven of sins already borne by Jesus on the cross, but for forgiveness and healing in the relationship. Salvation is no excuse for not asking for forgiveness when we have hurt God.

? How free do you feel to confess your sins to other people? How have you seen
• that confession truly brings you into deeper fellowship with God and with others? Do others know you believe in the power of confession?

19

Us and Them
1 JOHN 2

From death to life: What a metamorphosis! What more pointed way to describe the transition that takes place in a man or woman in the waters of baptism! Then why was it the false prophets were blurring the distinction? Had these ex-Christians forgotten what they had experienced in Christ? To quit the church, to leave the fellowship, to "go out," as John puts it—how could they do this? The unthinkable. "We happy few, we band of brothers" had become, roughly put, "us and them."

> *¹My dear children, I write this to you so that you will not sin. But if anybody does sin, we have one who speaks to the Father in our defense—Jesus Christ, the Righteous One. ²He is the atoning sacrifice for our sins, and not only for ours but also for the sins of the whole world.*

This is great news! Not that we should abuse God's kindness, but in case we do sin (and we all do, let's be honest), Jesus is right there speaking in our defense. Not rationalizing our sin through slick argument, but neutralizing it through his atoning blood. Would that the whole world grasped this and experienced it (2:2)!

> *³We know that we have come to know him if we obey his commands. ⁴The man who says, "I know him," but does not do what he commands is a liar, and the truth is not in him. ⁵But if anyone obeys his word, God's love is truly made complete in him. This is how we know we are in him: ⁶Whoever claims to live in him must walk as Jesus did.*

What a clear passage on the commitment the Lord requires! It silences the pious opposition of those who insist that uncommitted people can be saved. Walking as Jesus did is not

149

walking in sandals or walking on water. As we have seen, the
walking of 2:6 is equivalent to the walking of 1:7.

There is a tremendous difference between knowing someone and knowing about someone. According to Jesus (Matthew 7:21-23), countless individuals confuse knowing about
the Lord with knowing him *personally*. For example, one of the
better known celebrities I have met is Mother Teresa. We talked
for seven minutes. I held her hand for the first two minutes.
We exchanged business cards. We talked. Do I know about
her? Certainly. But do I really know her? Is there any real sort
of two-way relationship? No. So how can we be sure that we
really know God? Obedience is the key. (See also 1 Corinthians
8:3.)

John insists there is no contradiction between living as a
committed disciple and salvation by grace through the blood
of Jesus. Grace is designed to do one thing: bring us into an
obedient relationship with Christ. If we do not want to be obedient, we do not want what the very thing grace is designed to
bring. Real Christianity is a relationship with God first and
foremost, then with others. As in marriage, without commitment (faithfulness) the relationship sours and is eventually
destroyed.

? When do you most need to claim the promise of 1 John 2:1-2? How does obeying
. God lead to God's love being made complete in you? What is your attitude toward obedience?

> *⁷Dear friends, I am not writing you a new command but an
> old one, which you have had since the beginning. This old
> command is the message you have heard. ⁸Yet I am writing
> you a new command; its truth is seen in him and you, because
> the darkness is passing and the true light is already shining.*

The command about love was old (Deuteronomy 6:5;
Leviticus 19:18; Matthew 22:37-40) but also new because now
we can see clearly what we need to do by imitating God in the
flesh (John 13:34). The truth of this command is seen "in him
and you": in the life of Christ and in our life as his body, the
church of Christ.

The command to live as Jesus did is all about love (2:5),
because the disciple's life revolves around loving people. This
love shines as a bright light in a dark, selfish world.

⁹Anyone who claims to be in the light but hates his brother is still in the darkness. ¹⁰Whoever loves his brother lives in the light, and there is nothing in him to make him stumble. ¹¹But whoever hates his brother is in the darkness and walks around in the darkness; he does not know where he is going, because the darkness has blinded him.

Those who had left the fellowship did not love their brothers. It seems John is saying that those who leave the church, who do not keep their commitment of love to God and the family of God, "hate" their spiritual siblings. Certainly they hate them when push comes to shove, because they fight against the light and hate the straight talk and high standards of the true disciples. Light or darkness, truth or falsehood, love or hate: These are the antitheses, and there are no alternatives.

Do we love our brothers or not? Is there hidden resentment or prideful independence that resists correction? Prejudice or hatred in any other form? In 1 John 4:20 John insists that when this is the case, we are on the road to destruction.

¹²I write to you, dear children,
because your sins have been forgiven
on account of his name.

"Children" here is not referring to infants or toddlers. It is those of us who have become children of God through the new birth. "My dear children" is one of John's favorite descriptions of those who are in Christ. Our sins were forgiven through the name of Jesus, but when? At baptism, as Acts 2:38 and 22:16 make clear.

"The name" (2:12) represents the authority and nature of the individual. (See Exodus 6:3 and Deuteronomy 12:11.)

What rules are there for us to follow in the Bible in connection with baptism?

- Baptism is immersion (*baptisma*, "immersion").
- It must follow repentance (Acts 2:37). No retroactive validity!
- Its purpose is the forgiveness of sins (Acts 2:38).

• The confession "Jesus is Lord" is made (Romans 10:9). No further questions are needed.[1]

Baptism may be performed in "the name of the Father, Son and Holy Spirit" (Matthew 28:19-20) or in "the name of Jesus" (Acts 2:38) since reference in both cases is being made to the one God. Obviously the NT writers did not think there was one formula that excluded others.

> [13]*I write to you, fathers,*
> > *because you have known him who is*
> > > *from the beginning.*
> *I write to you, young men,*
> > *because you have overcome the evil one.*
> *I write to you, dear children,*
> > *because you have known the Father.*
> [14]*I write to you, fathers,*
> > *because you have known him who is*
> > > *from the beginning.*
> *I write to you, young men,*
> > *because you are strong,*
> > *and the word of God lives in you,*
> > *and you have overcome the evil one.*

The above is a powerful poem, or song, which became familiar to the first century Christians. The rhyme and rhythm are evident in the Greek original, which is why the NIV translators have set it out in verse form. The way to overcome the evil one is to let the word of Christ dwell in you (Colossians 3:16; Psalm 119:9). John assures us that the victory is ours! This being the case, we need to think of ourselves as overcomers.

---

[1] The baptismal verse Acts 8:37 ("Philip said, 'If you believe with all your heart, you may.' The Eunuch answered, 'I believe that Jesus Christ is the Son of God.'") is an insertion into the Greek text appearing in no manuscript before the sixth century and is not present in the best translations for that reason. Yet since it appears in the KJV and other versions, several groups have unwittingly been influenced by it in their pre-baptismal confession: "Do you believe that Jesus Christ is the Son of God? What is your good confession?" (the "two questions"). But do we really have a right to make such creedal requirements when there is no biblical precedent? The only biblical prerequisites for baptism are faith, repentance and the classic Christian confession, "Jesus is Lord" (Romans 10:9; 1 Timothy 6:12). No other questions, no matter how well intended, are binding.

> *[15]Do not love the world or anything in the world. If anyone loves the world, the love of the Father is not in him. [16]For everything in the world—the cravings of sinful man, the lust of his eyes and the boasting of what he has and does—comes not from the Father but from the world. [17]The world and its desires pass away, but the man who does the will of God lives forever.*

The warning about loving the world reminds us of James 4:4. We are to love nothing in the world because it is not possible to serve more than one master (Luke 16:13). What is "worldliness"? How do you define such a concept for someone without a spiritual bone in his body? *The worldly man thinks about everything in relation to himself; the godly man in relation to God.* And the bonus for the man who lives for God: eternal life. Those who had left the church for Docetic theology were, despite their religion, worldly to the core.

? What did you once love about the world? What is there is this world that still holds the greatest attraction for you? How does John's message help you deal with that?

> *[18]Dear children, this is the last hour; and as you have heard that the antichrist is coming, even now many antichrists have come. This is how we know it is the last hour. [19]They went out from us, but they did not really belong to us. For if they had belonged to us, they would have remained with us; but their going showed that none of them belonged to us.*

The false Christians left the fellowship. They stopped going to church—the right church, that is. They started up their own. As soon as that happened, it was "us and them."

The meaning of the "last hour" (2:18) is difficult to pin down. Maybe it refers to the end of the world, though this view is not without fairly obvious difficulties! It does, however, follow on smoothly from verse 17. If this is correct, are we still in the last hour? Did it come and go, or are we still "on stand-by" for the end? Some hold that it refers to the final years before the destruction of Jerusalem (Matthew 24), in which case these were the *final days of Judaism,* or Christianity within Judaism—enjoying imperial protection. Things would heat up considerably for the Christians after 70 A.D.! Perhaps it

alludes to final hour in the Parable of the Workers in the Vine-
yard (Matthew 20:12) and thus refers to the influx of Gentiles
into the Kingdom. Could it be that the Holy Spirit is revealing
that, for the Christians in Asia Minor, persecution will soon
eradicate the faith in that part of the world? In other words,
it's the "last hour" *locally,* not globally, for these disciples. On
the other hand, maybe this is a reference to Paul's prophecy (2
Timothy 4:3), or Jesus' oracle (Matthew 24.12-14, 24). Both
passages (and many others) speak of disciples being led away
from the truth.

Indeed, this is one of the more difficult passages of Scripture. We cannot be too dogmatic. Choose the view which best
commends itself to you. At any rate, *all* disciples must *always*
be ready for the end; Jesus promised he would come as a thief.

> *[20]But you have an anointing from the Holy One, and all of
> you know the truth. [21]I do not write to you because you do not
> know the truth, but because you do know it and because no lie
> comes from the truth. [22]Who is the liar? It is the man who
> denies that Jesus is the Christ. Such a man is the antichrist—
> he denies the Father and the Son. [23]No one who denies the Son
> has the Father; whoever acknowledges the Son has the Fa-
> ther also.*
>
> *[24]See that what you have heard from the beginning remains
> in you. If it does, you also will remain in the Son and in the
> Father. [25]And this is what he promised us—even eternal life.*
>
> *[26]I am writing these things to you about those who are try-
> ing to lead you astray. [27]As for you, the anointing you received
> from him remains in you, and you do not need anyone to teach
> you. But as his anointing teaches you about all things and as
> that anointing is real, not counterfeit—just as it has taught
> you, remain in him.*

Here begins one of the most difficult sections of the entire
NT (2:20-27). Endless discussion and wild speculations have
issued from loose and irresponsible study of these things. We
must touch on the concepts of "antichrist" and "anointing."

The antichrist is not necessarily one pernicious individual;
rather, many antichrists have come—those who deny the teachings of Christ and sacrificial lifestyle demanded of his followers.

"All of you know the truth (2:20)": The false teachers whom
John is refuting claimed that extra, esoteric, mystical knowledge was necessary in order to fully apprehend the truth. Gnosticism was a highly speculative religion-philosophy. John
counters by affirming that all Christians *already* have the truth.
Jesus had promised that the Spirit would see to that. (For two
incredibly useful verses, each one a promise made to the
apostles, see John 14:26 and 16:13.) We need no teacher. Not
that we need no teaching (!), but we have no need of someone
to come along and change or add to the gospel.

The "anointing" (2:20) refers the original, pristine, apostolic doctrine which is both immutable and inimitable. No
one needs to teach us the truth; we learned it when we first
came to know the Lord. Jeremiah 31:34 with Hebrews 8:10-11
continues this thought. 1 John 2:21 shows that "knowing the
truth" is equivalent to "receiving the anointing" (2:20, 27).
The liar rejects the sufficiency of this "anointing." He denies
that Jesus is the Messiah. The liar's teaching is counterfeit; it
resembles the genuine article, but look at it up close and its
cheapness, baseness and uselessness become evident.

In all likelihood these Gnostics have Jewish roots. Some
scholars suggest that when they "went out" from the church
they returned to the synagogue, where they would escape persecution (if only for a while). The false prophets (1 John 4:1-6)
would likely have permitted their adherents to worship in their
own way, even if that meant a return to established religion
(Judaism). However, there is no way to be saved apart from the
truth of Christ—and the Christ of truth (2:23).

> [28]*And now, dear children, continue in him, so that when he
> appears we may be confident and unashamed before him at
> his coming.*
> [29]*If you know that he is righteous, you know that everyone
> who does what is right has been born of him.*

"Confident and unashamed" (2:28): Is this how you would
stand before God if you were to be ushered into his presence
now? That's how we should feel and that's how we can feel
when we understand the power of Christ's cleansing blood (1
John 1:7-2:2). (See 3:19-21 for the continuation of this thought.)

Ironically, the false teachers were also confident (arrogantly so) and unashamed (though they should have been). But in verse 29 John reminds us that true Christians not only "talk right," they also "walk right." A sinful lifestyle is proof that the prophets are false (Matthew 7:15-20). Whether they'd (initially) crossed from death to life is irrelevant; they were now living for themselves. And when you live for self, the Bible says, you're dead even while you live (1 Timothy 5:6).

? What are some basic and powerful truths that you learned about Jesus when you first became a Christian that will continue to be powerful for you as long as you live? What most motivates you to want to do what is right?

20

I Wanna Know What Love Is
1 JOHN 3

In a culture where indulgence is exalted as "freedom," crime is called "sickness," lust is called "love" and "tolerance" is held in higher regard than honesty, it is not surprising that our musicians (who are the prophets and poets of our society), cry out "I wanna know what love is!" Love is a major theme in 1 John—no reader can miss it. What bothers modern man is its price tag: commitment. The fact is, our world wants to know what love is, and disciples need to show them! No one else will.

> *[1]How great is the love the Father has lavished on us, that we should be called children of God! And that is what we are! The reason the world does not know us is that it did not know him.*

From the mention of rebirth ("born of him," 1 John 2:29) John moves into praise for God and his love for us as his children. God lavishes it on us, since he wants us to have the abundant life. Then immediately he reminds us that the reason we are opposed by the world and its spokesmen (false prophets) is that they did not recognize Jesus.

> *[2]Dear friends, now we are children of God, and what we will be has not yet been made known. But we know that when he appears, we shall be like him, for we shall see him as he is. [3]Everyone who has this hope in him purifies himself, just as he is pure.*

When we actually see the Lord in the end, we will be *like* him. That much we know for certain. We know little else—because it has not been revealed in the Scriptures. No need to guess. Yet even the hope of seeing God helps to keep us pure.

That's because we live in the anticipation of seeing God: personally, directly and at any moment. And to meet him, we must be pure (Habakkuk 1:13).

> [4]*Everyone who sins breaks the law; in fact, sin is lawlessness.* [5]*But you know that he appeared so that he might take away our sins. And in him is no sin.* [6]*No one who lives in him keeps on sinning. No one who continues to sin has either seen him or known him.*

Verse 4 gives us a compact definition of sin. Sin is, in fact, transgression of God's moral law; a personal affront to God, not a violation of some arbitrary code. Taking morality into our own hands (as our generation has done), refusing to submit to the sovereignty of God and asserting our own autonomy or right to "interpret" the will of God: this is the epitome of lawlessness. The Gnostics sinned and sinned boldly. To them sin was a technicality, or some imperfection that they were above, since they considered themselves to be perfect. Jesus came to change all that.

Moreover, Jesus is sinless (John 8:46). Those who continue to sin have neither seen him (as he is) or known him (Matthew 7:23; 1 Corinthians 8:3). "Continuing to sin" (present tense in Greek—continuous action) means a lifestyle of unrepented of sinfulness, as in Hebrews 10:26, not isolated acts of sin.

? Imagine "Joe" who continues to sin. And then imagine "Jim" who also sins. What would cause God to view their sins in a totally different way, forgiving "Jim" but judging "Joe"? Are you a "Jim" or a "Joe"?

> [7]*Dear children, do not let anyone lead you astray. He who does what is right is righteous, just as he is righteous.* [8]*He who does what is sinful is of the devil, because the devil has been sinning from the beginning. The reason the Son of God appeared was to destroy the devil's work.* [9]*No one who is born of God will continue to sin, because God's seed remains in him; he cannot go on sinning, because he has been born of God.* [10]*This is how we know who the children of God are and who the children of the devil are: Anyone who does not do what is right is not a child of God; nor is anyone who does not love his brother.*

Satan will try to lead us astray through people. Fortunately, however, God's seed remains in us; we cannot go on sinning (living a lifestyle of sin). "Cannot" in the sense of our refusal, not our inability, since we always have free will. This seed is the seed of the Word (Luke 8:11), which we must retain (Luke 8:15). "Once saved, always saved" is again shown to be false doctrine!

> *[11]This is the message you heard from the beginning: We should love one another. [12]Do not be like Cain, who belonged to the evil one and murdered his brother. And why did he murder him? Because his own actions were evil and his brother's were righteous. [13]Do not be surprised, my brothers, if the world hates you.*

The false teachers bear an uncanny resemblance to Cain. Interestingly enough, some later antinomian Gnostics took Cain as their *hero!* The term "antinomian" means that they maintained a lawless position with regard to sin and righteousness (*anti* + *nomos* = against + law). They, like the false Christians of Romans 3 and 6, claimed that sinning magnified God's grace in forgiving sins.

> *[14]We know that we have passed from death to life, because we love our brothers. Anyone who does not love remains in death. [15]Anyone who hates his brother is a murderer, and you know that no murderer has eternal life in him.*
> *[16]This is how we know what love is: Jesus Christ laid down his life for us. And we ought to lay down our lives for our brothers. [17]If anyone has material possessions and sees his brother in need but has no pity on him, how can the love of God be in him? [18]Dear children, let us not love with words or tongue but with actions and in truth.*

True love is sacrificial. 1 John 3:16 has been described as "John 3:16 at the human level," and John 3:16 has been dubbed "1 John 3:16 at the divine level." Cain did not love Abel; rather than sacrificing in a godly manner, he "sacrificed" his own brother. Remember, towards the end of the first century more and more false Christians betrayed their spiritual brothers and sisters to death; turning in a Christian, especially a non-Roman citizen or a slave, would likely lead to the execution of that individual, assuming he refused to worship Caesar as Lord. So we see that one mark of the false Christian is his unwillingness to be persecuted, especially to be martyred.

But John gives us another easy test for true and false Christianity: *How do those who claim to be disciples sacrifice to meet the needs of those less fortunate?* For example, in India the disciples are reluctant to baptize anyone who expresses unwillingness to go into the slums, to reach out to the lepers, or to "get his hands dirty" in identifying with the poor and needy of this world. Such a person has not repented. If we are repulsed by imitating the love and work of Christ, how can we possibly identify with him in his sacrificial death? (See also James 2:14-26.)

? How does your living of 1 John 3:16 show that you understand and appreciate John 3:16? Name one person who powerfully feels the impact of your love.

> [19]*This then is how we know that we belong to the truth, and how we set our hearts at rest in his presence* [20]*whenever our hearts condemn us. For God is greater than our hearts, and he knows everything.*
> [21]*Dear friends, if our hearts do not condemn us, we have confidence before God* [22]*and receive from him anything we ask, because we obey his commands and do what pleases him.*

Setting our hearts at rest in God's presence, has been misunderstood to say that we should put our hearts at ease in God's presence apart from living the life of a disciple. Some religious people say anything that upsets you is wrong—anything that takes away "the peace of Christ" should be avoided. But, as it has often been quipped, "Jesus came to comfort the disturbed and to disturb the comfortable"!

Especially do those with sensitive consciences or more "accused" personalities find that "their hearts condemn them." If you don't have such struggles, do not make light of those who do. John even includes himself in those who have them. But he offers a solution. If we have committed ourselves to loving others and are laying down our lives for them, God sees our hearts, and he does not condemn us. We may have vague feelings of unworthiness, but our actions show where we really are.

What is John saying in this passage? When we love "with actions and in truth" (3:18) our hearts will be at rest before God because our *consciences* will be at peace! Attempts to feel good spiritually apart from discipleship are misguided at best. Here are three simple tests, each inherent in the message of 1 John, which we can apply:

- Do I actively seek to alleviate the suffering of the needy?
- Am I fulfilling my commission to spread the Word everywhere?
- Do I call my brothers and sisters in Christ to the same commitment?

And when our hearts are at rest, we receive what we want because we are focused and godly in our prayers. (See a similar thought in James 1:2-6.)

> [23]*And this is his command: to believe in the name of his Son, Jesus Christ, and to love one another as he commanded us.* [24]*Those who obey his commands live in him, and he in them. And this is how we know that he lives in us: We know it by the Spirit he gave us.*

Finally, we know he abides in us by the Spirit he gave us (3:24). Not because of some feeling we have (either because we can feel the Spirit or because the Spirit makes us feel good); but rather, we know the Lord is living in us because of the *effects* of his Spirit in us (practical love and other elements in the fruit of the Spirit). So to the extent that those effects are absent, Christ is not dwelling in us richly. The more we surrender to his Spirit, the more we will enjoy walking in the light—which is walking in his steps—and the more he will use us to spread the Word in this world.

They wanna know what love is. Will you show them?

? Who is someone who has clearly shown you what love is? Who are some people in your life right now who need to know what love is? What can you do today to show them the love of God?

21

Love, Not Lies
1 JOHN 4

At times it's nearly impossible to soften the truth. While occasionally the truth is "a shade of gray," many truths are simply black and white. If we lie to ourselves and to others about our relationship with God, we will be punished at the Last Day instead of being rewarded. The acid test for our relationship with God is not: how many hours we pray, how many people we invite or even how many midweek church services we attend. No, the acid test is *our relationships with others*. As John puts it in 1 John 4:20, if we claim to love the (invisible) Lord while we don't love our (visible) brother, we lie. And if we lie, we fry (Revelation 21:8). That's straight talk, but it's true. It is far better to love than to lie.

> *¹Dear friends, do not believe every spirit, but test the spirits to see whether they are from God, because many false prophets have gone out into the world. ²This is how you can recognize the Spirit of God: Every spirit that acknowledges that Jesus Christ has come in the flesh is from God, ³but every spirit that does not acknowledge Jesus is not from God. This is the spirit of the antichrist, which you have heard is coming and even now is already in the world.*

The term "spirits" (4:1) in this passage is equivalent to "prophetic messages." The same word "spirit" is rendered "prophecy" in 2 Thessalonians 2:2, thus making the whole idea akin to 1 Thessalonians 5:20-21. The point: Don't be easily duped by false charismatics. God's true Spirit always works in harmony with God's word and will never teach, tolerate or lead us into error of any kind.

> *⁴You, dear children, are from God and have overcome them, because the one who is in you is greater than the one who is in the world. ⁵They are from the world and therefore speak from*

the viewpoint of the world, and the world listens to them. ⁶We are from God, and whoever knows God listens to us; but whoever is not from God does not listen to us. This is how we recognize the Spirit of truth and the spirit of falsehood.

The world, including pagans, worldly religious persons and everyone who accepts worldly thinking and excuses approves of the false prophets (1 John 3:5) with their compromised message and compromising lifestyle. It can be frustrating to know the truth but feel powerless to bring others to repentance. Don't we as disciples sometimes fret when we fail to change people—either non-Christians we are trying to influence for Christ or Christians who are proving to be "rocky" or "thorny" soil (Matthew 13; Mark 4; Luke 8)?

Yet the problem is not always that we are doing a poor job explaining the gospel, or that our faith is too "narrow." In fact John assures us this is a normal part of Christian life. There are two sides, two basic viewpoints, two roads (Matthew 7:13-14, 15-20). Bottom line, anyone who understands our position and rejects us is lost. It's that person, not us, who is in the darkness. Be confident; as long as we are following Jesus, we do not need to worry about our opponents. Anyone on the side of truth will join us in the movement of God, the quest for pure Christianity and the conviction that the Bible must be studied and obeyed by all on a daily basis.

? When are you most tempted to think that darkness may be getting the better of light? When are the times when you most need to remember that "the one who is in you is greater than the one that is in the world"?

⁷Dear friends, let us love one another, for love comes from God. Everyone who loves has been born of God and knows God. ⁸Whoever does not love does not know God, because God is love. ⁹This is how God showed his love among us: He sent his one and only Son into the world that we might live through him. ¹⁰This is love: not that we loved God, but that he loved us and sent his Son as an atoning sacrifice for our sins. ¹¹Dear friends, since God so loved us, we also ought to love one another.

Love is the very nature of God, and it is impossible to understand real love without appreciating the cross of Christ. In

the Greek language there are four types of love. (For more on
this, see C.S. Lewis, *The Four Loves*.)

Greek	Definition	Usual translation
philia	friendship	Love, friendship
storge	family affection	Love, affection
eros	sexual love	Love, passion
agape	sacrificial love	Love, charity

Agape, the type of love always mentioned in 1 John, is de-
fined by God's action in Christ Jesus—not by theologians, psy-
chologists or even real-life heroes who provide us with flesh-
and-blood examples. *Agape* is not a feeling, it's a commitment.
It's deeper than friendship and deeper even than family bonds,
as close as they are. *Agape* will not be found in pseudo-Christian denominations—even those who say they believe in the
whole Bible—because their lack of discipleship, directness and
honesty at the personal level shows that they don't understand
the cross at a deep heart-level.

> [12]No one has ever seen God; but if we love one another, God
> lives in us and his love is made complete in us.
> [13]We know that we live in him and he in us, because he has
> given us his Spirit. [14]And we have seen and testify that the
> Father has sent his Son to be the Savior of the world. [15]If any-
> one acknowledges that Jesus is the Son of God, God lives in
> him and he in God.

No one has ever fully, exhaustively seen God (John 1:18;
Isaiah 55:8-9), though at times God has made one aspect or
another of himself visible (Exodus 34, for example). Certainly
we see God in the person of Jesus as recorded in the Bible
(Colossians 2:9). But today Jesus is at the right hand of the
Father and through his spirit he lives in his body, the church
(Ephesians 1:22-23, 2:22). So, although God is invisible, he
may be seen in Christian relationships. God means for the
world to see him through his Son in the church. That's why
it's so hard to lead someone to Christ without his or her visit-
ing church. In other words, it is difficult for someone to believe in God when he hasn't seen him!
    People can dismiss you, one person, as an unusually com-
mitted Christian, but they cannot so easily dismiss an entire

congregation of giving, zealous, loving disciples! God never meant for Christianity to be a solo event; it's a *team* sport. Life to the full is not a private, mystical experience; *it's only possible in a community* (the church). So keep bringing your friends to the meetings, and let them see the fellowship.

> [16]*And so we know and rely on the love God has for us. God is love. Whoever lives in love lives in God, and God in him.* [17]*In this way, love is made complete among us so that we will have confidence on the day of judgment, because in this world we are like him.* [18]*There is no fear in love. But perfect love drives out fear, because fear has to do with punishment. The one who fears is not made perfect in love.*

"No Fear" is a popular brand name and a motto sometimes emblazoned on clothing. Is this your personal motto? Do you walk confidently before God and man? A more important question: Will "No Fear" also be your confidence at the judgment? "Fear has to do with punishment" (4:18): Christians know they're forgiven, and perfect (mature, complete) love drives out fear. We revere God (a good sort of fear), but we don't stand in terror of God (the *bad* sort) for three reasons:

- We are already acquainted with him (he is no stranger), and we are confident about his unchanging nature. We may feel nervous about an encounter with some authority figure we have never met, but once there is trust and a relationship, there is no cause for fear. Ultimately this means that a disciple need not fear death. We do not fear him because *we know him.*
- God has assured us in Christ that he will do anything to get us to heaven. The cross is a sufficiently loud statement of his heart; we should never doubt God's intentions for us. "For God did not send his Son into the world to condemn the world, but to save the world through him" (John 3:17).
- He has set our hearts at peace, forgiving us and providing us with the gift of a good conscience (Hebrews 9:14). Moreover, when we are living right, our hearts will automatically be at rest (the "default setting" of a disciple!).

Another question is: What will the judgment day be like for Christians? Will our lives be reviewed in order to determine whether we go to heaven or hell or merely to determine some level of reward in heaven? Space forbids going into this in detail here, so let me remind you of some of the basic facts, and you can begin to work out your own conclusion:

- All disciples will appear before the judgment seat (2 Corinthians 5:10).
- At his return Christ will bring salvation to those waiting for him (Hebrews 9:28).
- We are not saved by our works (Ephesians 2:8-9), but we are rewarded according to our works (Matthew 25:21).
- Jesus frequently mentions treasures in heaven (Matthew 6:20).
- Punishment, like reward, is in direct proportion to knowledge and responsibility (Luke 12:47-48). It just is not true that all get the same reward or punishment.
- We can know we are saved (1 John 5:13) and thus be confident and unashamed before God at his coming (1 John 2:28).
- At the return of Christ we will receive the gift of eternal life (1 Corinthians 15:50, 53).
- At that time we will not only meet Jesus Christ, but we will finally reach our goal and become fully like him (1 John 3:2).

? How does "no fear" characterize your life? What fear does God still want to help you overcome?

> [19]We love because he first loved us. [20]If anyone says, "I love God," yet hates his brother, he is a liar. For anyone who does not love his brother, whom he has seen, cannot love God, whom he has not seen. [21]And he has given us this command: Whoever loves God must also love his brother.

Many people talk about their "personal" relationship with God. They claim to be "born again," though they don't exactly *live* like "new creations." Judged by their defensiveness, worldliness and bitterness towards friends, enemies, family and others, their lack of love is noticeable. If they have crossed anywhere, it is from life to death.

It is not logically possible to love God (who is *invisible*) if you do not love your brothers and sisters (who are *visible*). Imagine a surgeon doing an operation blind: unthinkable! Are you a surgeon? Probably not. So what chance would you have of successfully completing an operation blindfolded? Even less than with open eyes. Imagine cycling, or driving, with your eyes closed! Let's admit the simple point: Everything is far, far easier when we see what we are doing!

When people say they love the invisible God, while it's clear that they have significant difficulty loving their visible neighbors, something is wrong: They are lying (according to John). Here are some clear contradictions to the claim that we love God, all of which bring reproach on the Christian church:

- Bitterness and resentment (Hebrews 12:15).
- Racism and prejudice, which are forms of hatred (Galatians 5:20).
- Segregated churches. It has been accurately observed, "11:00 on Sunday morning is the most segregated hour of the week."
- Those who do not seek unity with true disciples but rather, contribute to denominationalism (1 Corinthians 1:10-12, 3:16-17; John 17:20-23).
- Fragmenting or fractured marriages (Ephesians 5:22-33).
- Unloving treatment of others, violating the spirit of 1 Corinthians 13:1-8.
- Lack of forgiveness, which is damnable (Matthew 6:14-15).

Love is the bottom line. A true Christian must love his God (relationship with God), love his brothers and sisters (church) and actively love the lost (evangelism). These truths we hold to be (biblically) self-evident.

Don't lie; tell the truth. Live the truth. And if the truth means you need to change, get going! Live a life of love.

? Look carefully at the above list of those things that contradict the love of God. Which of these is the greatest challenge in your life? Pray about three people in your life to whom you want to show the love of God today.

22

The *Other* Easy Way
1 John 5

Two of the most encouraging verses in the Bible are found in 1 John 5. The first is verse 3, which promises that God's commands are not burdensome (in other words, "life to the full" isn't only a theoretical possibility, but is actually in reach for all who want it). The second is verse 13, which tells us we can absolutely know whether we are saved or not. How the religious world would be transformed if only it understood these two teachings! So, though we should avoid the "easy road" (Matthew 7:13), the way of God is *another* easy way (Matthew 11:28-30), if our attitude is right. And why make things harder than they are?

> *[1]Everyone who believes that Jesus is the Christ is born of God, and everyone who loves the father loves his child as well. [2]This is how we know that we love the children of God: by loving God and carrying out his commands.*

It is not possible to accept God while rejecting the biblical Jesus. When we are close to someone, and that person becomes a parent, we rejoice with them in their child. The Gnostics took little pleasure in the real, historical Jesus—a clear sign they did not have a relationship with God. (See also John 3:18.)

> *[3]This is love for God: to obey his commands. And his commands are not burdensome, [4]for everyone born of God overcomes the world. This is the victory that has overcome the world, even our faith. [5]Who is it that overcomes the world? Only he who believes that Jesus is the Son of God.*

Loving God means obeying his commandments. (See also John 14:15, 23-24.) A so-called Christian who cannot say sincerely, "I'm a disciple of Jesus. I am striving daily to obey his commands" is not right with God. Biblically speaking, it is unthinkable that one could be faithful to God while being willfully disobedient to him.

And the good news: his commands are not burdensome, when kept out of a faithful heart. In Deuteronomy 30:11-20 God has assured the Israelites of the same thing. His commands are not burdensome; obeying them lifts the burden. Obeying them lifts the burden of sin, bad relationships, meaningless living—just to mention a few. That must be what John means when he talks about a faith that overcomes the world. Real faith really leads to obedience, and obedience to God leads to victory over the empty way of life the world offers (see 1 Peter 1:18).

? When do God's commands begin to seem burdensome to you? When do they not seem burdensome to you at all? Does it have more to do with the command or more to do with your heart?

⁶This is the one who came by water and blood—Jesus Christ. He did not come by water only, but by water and blood. And it is the Spirit who testifies, because the Spirit is the truth. ⁷For there are three that testify: ⁸the Spirit, the water and the blood; and the three are in agreement. ⁹We accept man's testimony, but God's testimony is greater because it is the testimony of God, which he has given about his Son. ¹⁰Anyone who believes in the Son of God has this testimony in his heart. Anyone who does not believe God has made him out to be a liar, because he has not believed the testimony God has given about his Son. ¹¹And this is the testimony: God has given us eternal life, and this life is in his Son. ¹²He who has the Son has life; he who does not have the Son of God does not have life.

John assures us that to enjoy the Christian life, we must have the correct Christ first. This may sound a bit strange, but if you take a look at 2 Corinthians 11:3-4 you will get the idea. Jesus came by water and blood: likely referring to his humanity, also likely an allusion to John 19:34, where, while hanging dead on the cross, both blood and water gush from Jesus' side when the Roman soldier pierces it.

¹³I write these things to you who believe in the name of the Son of God so that you may know that you have eternal life.

Can we know we are saved? Is it "arrogant" to claim we are on the narrow road? Is it wrong to "judge" our own salvation? Not according to John! Disciples who are eager to sacrifice for Jesus Christ know that a saving faith is an active faith (James 2:14-26). They learn to accept God's grace, struggling less and less with trusting Christ for eternal life, ever growing in confidence.[1] The Bible is clear: you can absolutely know you are saved!

> *[14]This is the confidence we have in approaching God: that if we ask anything according to his will, he hears us. [15]And if we know that he hears us—whatever we ask—we know that we have what we asked of him.*

How can we be sure God will answer our prayers? John says that we will receive anything we ask for if it is according to his will. Against this truth, the modern "Word-Faith" movement, as well as most of the neo-pentecostal charismatic movement, teach that if you believe it, presumably regardless of how God feels about it, it will happen. This is based on Mark 11:24 (taken out of context) and the living spirit of paganism which says that we can manipulate the gods.

? How much confidence do you have in approaching God? If there is little faith involved in your prayers, what will be the outcome of those prayers?

> *[16]If anyone sees his brother commit a sin that does not lead to death, he should pray and God will give him life. I refer to those whose sin does not lead to death. There is a sin that leads to death. I am not saying that he should pray about that. [17]All wrongdoing is sin, and there is sin that does not lead to death.*

What is "the sin that leads to death" (5:16)? In the context of 1 John, it is probably related to the errors of Gnosticism in rejecting the true Christ and falling away (see Hebrews 6:4-6). James tells us that death is the end-result of full-grown sin (James 1:13-15). To simplify a potentially long discussion, let's

---

[1] Ironically, religious persons without "works" often insist loudest that works are somehow not necessary, whereas those with the works know how crucial they are. Many erroneous theologies have been spun to protect people from the demands of biblical discipleship.

put it this way: We can be forgiven for any sin that we will repent of, but if someone is unwilling to repent, it won't help to pray for their forgiveness. This solid biblical principle is also found in Jeremiah 11:14 and 14:11.

> [18]*We know that anyone born of God does not continue to sin; the one who was born of God keeps him safe, and the evil one cannot harm him.* [20]*We know also that the Son of God has come and has given us understanding, so that we may know him who is true. And we are in him who is true—even in his Son Jesus Christ. He is the true God and eternal life.*

Being born again means that we will not continue to sin (5:18). This does not mean that we will never sin, but that, as disciples, we will not continue in a sinful lifestyle. Hebrews 10:26 explains this teaching.

We can be confident that we will be kept safe from the evil one (5:18). Like all assurances of salvation in the Bible, this one, too, is conditional. John is not going back on his word that we must walk in the light (1:7), confess sin (1:9), obey the commandments and follow Jesus (2:3-6) and love our brother (4:19-21), etc.

> [19]*We know that we are children of God, and that the whole world is under the control of the evil one.*

The whole world is under the control of the evil one. Exactly how Satan controls the world through his spiritual forces (Ephesians 6:10-12) is never spelled out—despite hundreds of works in the religious bookstores speculating on and describing the exact mechanisms! It is certain, however, that he has considerable dominion over the earth. No one but a true disciple escapes his control.

> [21]*Dear children, keep yourselves from idols.*

This striking final verse fits well with the theme of 1 John. What are the "idols" which he warns us against if not the false concepts of Jesus and God taught by the Gnostics? A wrong-headed concept of Jesus is a dangerous thing: by it a man or

woman will be lost just as surely as by the true Jesus a man or
woman will be saved. Anyone who seriously wants life to the
full will keep himself from idols.

Wrap-up

That's straight talk. You'll hear more of it as we move on
and study 2 John and 3 John. In short, it is easy to be lost when
your heart isn't right, but it is also easy to be saved when you
just want to love and obey God....Amen! That's good news!

? Why must you have a deep conviction that "the whole world is under the control of
the evil one"? What idols have you dethroned in your life? Which ones are the
greatest threat to you even now? What do you hear as the overriding message of
this letter from John?

23

"Progressive" Theology
2 JOHN

S econd John is the shortest document in the New Testament, even shorter than Third John, also written by John the "elder." On closer inspection it clearly deals with the same situation addressed by 1 John—the spreading influence of Docetic Gnosticism among the churches of the eastern Roman Empire. And though the letter is short, it's meaty.[1]

> [1]The elder,
> To the chosen lady and her children, whom I love in the truth—and not I only, but also all who know the truth—[2]because of the truth, which lives in us and will be with us forever:

"The elder" is the apostle John, son of Zebedee, brother of James, friend of Jesus. An elder could technically be in his 30s or 40s if he had children who were believers (Titus 1:6), yet the feel we get from this greeting is that John is in his latter years.

Who is the "chosen lady"? Scholars are divided. Either she is an actual woman, or, like "she who is in Babylon" of 1 Peter 5:13, another church. It is my view that she is a church. In this case, the "children" in the final verse are church members, and her "sister" is a sister congregation.

In verse 2 John is emphatic that his readers already have the truth. In other words, they don't need some teacher of secret wisdom coming in and showing them what real spirituality is.

---

[1] For your information, the shortest chapter in the OT is Psalm 117; the longest in the whole Bible is Psalm 119. The shortest verse in the whole Bible? Probably a tie between 1 Chronicles 1:1 and John 11:35 which each have three words in the original languages.

³Grace, mercy and peace from God the Father and from Jesus Christ, the Father's Son, will be with us in truth and love.
⁴It has given me great joy to find some of your children walking in the truth, just as the Father commanded us.

Notice John's remark about grace. Grace is "with us in truth and love." False grace talks much about love and little about truth. Saving grace integrates truth *and* love. He is setting up for his warning against the heretics, just a few verses away.

"The children" are children of God, disciples who refused to allow themselves to be influenced by the false teachers. They are walking in obedience, walking in God's commands. True freedom is not found in a corrupt lifestyle, but in doing what is right, as John proceeds to clarify.

⁵And now, dear lady, I am not writing you a new command but one we have had from the beginning. I ask that we love one another. ⁶And this is love: that we walk in obedience to his commands. As you have heard from the beginning, his command is that you walk in love.

"Love" sounds so simple, and false teachers like to use the word to attract a following. But real love has a price. Precious few people understand love, which is why even disciples have so much to learn about relationships. The opponents of the faith did not walk in love. They may have been ever so religious, but the message of the Bible is that religion without love is worse than no religion at all (Matthew 9:13)! When Christians say that real faith boils down to one thing, love, here is what they mean:

- Wholehearted love for God (Deuteronomy 6:6; Matthew 22:36-38). This means there is no higher priority in life than the Cross of Christ. God's kingdom and his righteousness are everything (Matthew 6:33). Are you wholehearted? If not, you are falling down on the most important commandment.
- Love of neighbor (Matthew 26:39). This means fervent fellowship, fervent evangelism, fervent care for the poor and fervent family life. How involved are you? Do you truly love others, or merely wish them well? (James 2:16).

? What is one personal change that you could make that would enable you to love
others more powerfully?

*[7]Many deceivers, who do not acknowledge Jesus Christ as
coming in the flesh, have gone out into the world. Any such
person is the deceiver and the antichrist.*

This is a clear allusion to the Docetists (see Chapter 17 of
this book). Since they teach wrongly about Christ, resisting
the spirit, truth and commitment of his message, they are
antichrists. Any such person is the antichrist. These people are
deceivers. Wittingly or unwittingly, they twist the truth. They
have a conspiracy going, a conspiracy to suppress the truth
reminiscent of Romans 1. Here are some tenets the deceivers
hold dear:

• Whatever version of truth we preach, we must not upset
  people.
• Religion must keep within reasonable limits in its claims
  on our commitment.
• Religion should not foster openness between members;
  personal questions are off-limits.
• One "interpretation" is as good as another because there
  is no such thing as absolute truth.

*[8]Watch out that you do not lose what you have worked for, but
that you may be rewarded fully.*

Our full reward is in heaven. There are degrees of reward
in heaven, just as there are degrees of punishment in hell. Yet
even on this earth, it is possible to merely *exist,* not live life to
the full. Many things can steal our joy, from laziness to personal finances that are out of control to unresolved conflict to
lack of evangelism to badly mannered children. Get this clear:
God wants you to have a great life even in the midst of challenging circumstances. Anything that jeopardizes your joy requires your utmost attention.

*[9]Anyone who runs ahead and does not continue in the teach-
ing of Christ does not have God; whoever continues in the
teaching has both the Father and the Son.*

The false teachers "ran ahead." (Where did they think they were going?) Their "sophisticated" version of the gospel appealed to the arrogant. As a system, Gnosticism was fairly difficult to grasp, and members were initiated into many levels of enlightenment. You know you are running ahead when you cannot explain your convictions to the common man and when the basics of your faith are too complex for anyone without an advanced degree to grasp.

Highly theological and philosophical versions of Christianity are common today. They hold on to a little bit of the gospel, but most of their beliefs are human speculation. Discretion discourages me from writing out a long, doleful list of such groups. Colossians 2:8 comes to mind:

> See to it that no one takes you captive through hollow and deceptive philosophy, which depends on human tradition and the basic principles of this world rather than on Christ.

About Seminary

One way many clergymen get ahead of themselves is the partial study of theology—the seminary experience. My time at divinity school was productive (choose your courses carefully!), but I saw many students whose faith upon entering was ridiculed and "shrunk to size" after just one semester of study. No surprise that few clergymen preach with conviction; they actually lost their faith at seminary!

The basic problem is that professors focus far more on the claims of critics than on the message of the Bible. Questions are raised at such a pace that there is little time to answer them before the next barrage of criticisms of Christianity is leveled. Soon students learn to give the acceptable answer rather than fight through the issues themselves. (It is quicker and seems more likely to yield the desired 'A.')

The indoctrination process appeals to the ego because it gives the seminarian the illusion that he is privy to the "real facts" about Christianity. Consider some of the beliefs urged in most seminaries today—I name only a few teachings.

"Progressive" Seminary Teaching

- The OT creation, flood and miracle stories are nothing but ignorant mythology.
- Truth is relative, and tolerance is even more important than truth.
- The Bible is the word of man. Or it "bears witness to the word of God." Or it "contains the word of God."
- Apparent discrepancies in the biblical accounts should be considered contradictions. Attempts at harmonizing them are misguided, not progressive.
- Morality and ethics are personal value judgments. Right and wrong change depending on culture, century and situation.
- The gospel accounts were fabricated by the church generations after the events happened.
- Jesus' resurrection was a figurative, not literal resurrection. (His message lived on, faith in him made a comeback, etc.)
- If there is a God, he wouldn't condemn anyone. Most people will go to heaven.
- Since we're all prone to error, sin should not be exposed.
- We don't need to evangelize the other world religions; we need "dialogue" with them!
- The major prophets are Freud, Darwin and Sagan (not Isaiah, Jeremiah and Ezekiel); we should take our cues from them.
- Jesus' death on the cross was very meaningful, but it "saved" no one, because salvation is an outmoded concept. Modern men and women need assurance that they are okay as they are, not challenge to change.

Of course each of these views is erroneous and can be refuted, but few people have the background, Bible knowledge, time, desire or patience to work through them all while trying to graduate with a decent grade point average.[2]

---

[2] Not every institution that bears the name "seminary" would agree to these teachings. Certainly there are still seminaries that are committed to an evangelical message that would reject these ideas as strongly as I do. However, what you find here represents the trend found not only in mainline Protestant denominations but in Catholicism as well.

Tens of thousands of men and women have been ruined by their seminary education. I'm not saying we should discourage learning or avoid education. I'm not even saying ministers of the gospel should not have some degree of biblical and theological training—they actually need it! I am writing to warn you of what is pushed on would-be ministers in most seminaries. Even the conservative seminaries admit that they spend an inordinate amount of time studying the opinions of the liberals, instead of really giving their students a practical handle on the Bible.

Be careful. Watch what you read and what sort of teaching appeals to you. Don't flatter your ego. *Don't run ahead.* For when we get more "progressive" than Jesus, we have no salvation!

? In what ways are you tempted to make the gospel more "sophisticated"? Do you ever find yourself being ashamed of some biblical teaching? What message would John bring to us in such times?

[10]If anyone comes to you and does not bring this teaching, do not take him into your house or welcome him. [11]Anyone who welcomes him shares in his wicked work.

You can feel John's burning conviction! Don't welcome them! Have nothing to do with them! Don't make deals with them! ("Let's agree to disagree and not bring up anything unpleasant;" "I won't 'judge' you if you won't bad-mouth me to your friends.")

[12]I have much to write to you, but I do not want to use paper and ink. Instead, I hope to visit you and talk with you face to face, so that our joy may be complete.

John will continue this discussion when he arrives. Some things are better said face-to-face than over the telephone or in a letter. As always, his prime concern is their spiritual welfare and happiness.

[13]The children of your chosen sister send their greetings.

The church at which John is ministering (their "chosen sister") sends greetings via John to the church to which he is writing. We need relationships not just within our own local fellowship, but also with other disciples around the world. Do you have some special friends in other churches? In other nations? The church of the living God is a worldwide family, and that sense of family should not only permeate our fellowship at the local level, but span the globe.

Wrap-up

The gospel is simple. There are many "false prophets" out there (1 John 4:1). Their version of the truth, though it may sound progressive and in step with the times, is merely pandering to the spirit of the world. So don't "run ahead." Don't lag behind, either! Keep in step with the Spirit.

John's third letter is the subject of our next chapter. Get ready for more "straight talk" from the apostle of love.

? What is your best guard against "false prophets"?

24

"Personality Conflict"
3 JOHN

Family—(that is what the church is. If we have conflict in our own biological families, as small as they are, certainly we should expect conflict in our spiritual family! The church is a very large family, with potentially millions of relationships among very human and fallible individuals. So if you've been through some tension lately, or been on either the sending or the receiving end of selfishness, don't be surprised!

Some friction inevitably arises because of poor communication. But another kind of friction is much more insidious and harmful. The Bible calls it "dissensions" and "factions" (Galatians 5:20). This *always* results directly from sin. This is the situation 3 John addresses. It is serious, and it must be dealt with swiftly. Welcome to the world of Demetrius and Diotrephes.

> *¹The elder,*
> *To my dear friend Gaius, whom I love in the truth.*

This is a personal letter, of typical length. It only appears short compared to the other letters in the NT. After all, how often do you receive a 15-20 page letter, even in the age of word processors? Writing a letter was a much bigger undertaking in the first century. Ink (verse 13) was made from a compound of charcoal and vegetable gum. The papyrus was rolled up like a scroll, and a single leaf would have been enough to contain a letter like 2- or 3 John.

The mention of "truth" in this verse is setting us up for the fundamental problem: the struggle between truth and falsehood, good and evil, light and darkness. Gaius is on the side of truth, and in fact, it is possible to have friendship as God intended it only when truth is the basis of the relationship. This is why the fellowship of disciples of Christ intimidates outsiders; worldly relationships are not built on truth, and darkness is afraid of light (John 3:19-21).

> [2] *Dear friend, I pray that you may enjoy good health and that all may go well with you, even as your soul is getting along well.*

Perhaps Gaius (a common Roman name) was, like John, getting on in years. At any rate, John has a legitimate concern for Gaius' health.

Physical health and spiritual health are both important, and both are legitimate subjects for prayer. Some people stress spirituality to the point of neglecting the physical. Sacrifice is part and parcel of following Christ, but what good is it if we run ourselves into the ground? Jesus saw the need for the balance (Mark 6:31). At the other extreme, there are those who talk about the spiritual but whose first love is physical comfort and health.

Additionally, some disciples seem to think that Jesus would have disapproved of red meat and alcohol (ignoring all the scriptures to the contrary). They are full of suggestions of a rather green and vegetarian nature, of highly dubious theological merit. So, what can be recommended for all disciples, regardless of culture?

- Regular exercise. You will feel better, relate to others better and build character. It takes time, but the rewards are considerable.
- Bodily fitness. How is your physique? Excess weight is a poor testimony to "the disciplined life."
- Periodic medical and dental check-ups. Don't think it's somehow more spiritual to ignore them! Remember, Luke was a doctor!
- A reasonable night's sleep. Burn the midnight oil when necessary and with joy, but get enough rest to stay buoyant and vibrant. Avoid the extremes of asceticism and sloth!

Is this just a health advisory? Not at all. Recall that the Gnostics (assuming, with most scholars, that Diotrephes, whose name will appear shortly, was in such a group) totally misunderstood the balance and proper relationship between spirit and matter. John has the balance.

? Write down one or two things that you can do to improve the condition of your body. Who have you asked to encourage and support you in these things?

> *³It gave me great joy to have some brothers come and tell about your faithfulness to the truth and how you continue to walk in the truth. ⁴I have no greater joy than to hear that my children are walking in the truth.*

This reminds us of 2 John 4. "Continuing to walk in truth" here means not just "being faithful" but taking a stand amid the flood of heresy and compromise.

> *⁵Dear friend, you are faithful in what you are doing for the brothers, even though they are strangers to you. ⁶They have told the church about your love. You will do well to send them on their way in a manner worthy of God. ⁷It was for the sake of the Name that they went out, receiving no help from the pagans.*

Gaius is a mature, solid Christian. His love extends even to those he does not know personally (Colossians 1:28-2:1). Verse 6 clearly means that the brothers who came from John, probably the ones delivering this letter, should be provided financial support by the fellowship of which Gaius is part.

"The Name" (verse 7) refers to Jesus Christ, who is God. As far as support goes, ministers of the gospel should not compromise themselves by becoming dependent on the contributions of the worldly. Whoever "pulls the purse-strings" has an enormous effect on the strength of the ministry. "No help from the pagans" (verse 7) is a good policy today as well, especially in a religious world where the unscrupulous solicit funds from the gullible in order to finance their extravagant lifestyles. Asking the lost for money for the benefit of the poor is one thing; becoming dependent on them for one's salary is quite another.

> *⁸We ought therefore to show hospitality to such men so that we may work together for the truth.*

Hospitality is a highly lauded virtue in both Old and New Testaments. Inns in ancient times are reputed to have been squalid, in both the hygienic and moral senses of the word. Therefore, visitors to the region would stay with families, who considered it a great honor and an opportunity to provide the best they could offer to their valued guests.

⁹I wrote to the church, but Diotrephes, who loves to be first, will have nothing to do with us. ¹⁰So if I come, I will call attention to what he is doing, gossiping maliciously about us. Not satisfied with that, he refuses to welcome the brothers. He also stops those who want to do so and puts them out of the church.

John had already written to the church, but his letter fell on deaf ears as far as the faction of Diotrephes was concerned. (The letter was a common apostolic tool for enforcing unity, spreading truth and staying in touch.)

Diotrephes was a leader who enjoyed leadership too much. His sin was the sin of Satan at the dawn of time. He could not stand what he perceived to be competition, and in the spirit of Absalom (2 Samuel), strove to influence others to idolize him while viewing others with a suspicious eye. This was not a case of "personality conflict." It was pure, egotistical arrogance. To the disciple of Jesus, "incompatibility" and "personality conflict" are transparent rationalizations for sin.

Is this an un-Christian case of name-calling? The denominational world has overreacted; this is neither "unkind" nor unbiblical. In the Bible, influential opponents of the truth were often named publicly as a safeguard for the people of God. To refuse to expose them would be to allow their influence to increase; it would be the unloving thing to do. Certainly the names of Korah, Alexander, Judas, Hymeneus and Philetus deserved open condemnation! Obviously to mention from the pulpit the name of an individual whose impact on the church of God is minimal is wholly unnecessary and without biblical precedent.

? Is there any relationship in your life that you might tend to describe as a "personality conflict"? What role is sin playing in this situation? Who can help you in determining this?

> *¹¹Dear friend, do not imitate what is evil but what is good. Anyone who does what is good is from God. Anyone who does what is evil has not seen God.*

It is completely fair to assess a person's character on the basis of his or her outward life. When will the world learn that it's ridiculous to pretend that someone's private life has no organic connection with his or her public life? Politicians, statesmen, teachers, counselors, church leaders (all must be held to the same standards at home that they profess out of the home.

> *¹²Demetrius is well spoken of by everyone—and even by the truth itself. We also speak well of him, and you know that our testimony is true.*

How does the truth "speak"? Demetrius' life was in line with the truth of the gospel. His personal example was sterling. And how is your own example? Could anyone accuse you of corruption or even a trace of lukewarmness? (Daniel 6:4) It is that simple. Each person's life produces fruit (actions and words) and by their fruits you will know them (Matthew 7:20). The contrast is obvious: the broad road and the narrow road, the dominion of darkness and the kingdom of light, life and death. And God desires that we "choose life" (Deuteronomy 30:19). That should be a simple enough decision for those who have crossed over from death to life!

3 John gives us insight into the development of denominations. Considering Jesus' Gethsemane prayer that his church never divide (John 17), denominationalism is lamentable, unbiblical and inexcusable. But in the worldly mindset, it is acceptable. "The more options the better," the religious world proclaims. "The human spirit must not be 'fettered' by rules and authority; personal autonomy is salvation." 1 John 4:5-6 tells us to expect worldly men and women to excuse compromise and minimize the seriousness of division.

> *¹³I have much to write you, but I do not want to do so with pen and ink. ¹⁴I hope to see you soon, and we will talk face to face.*
>
> *Peace to you. The friends here send their greetings. Greet the friends there by name.*

John would visit soon enough and bring this matter to reso-
lution. Hopefully this brief note would sober up the trouble-
makers, "snatch others from the fire" (Jude 23) and put the
fear of God into the hearts of all the congregation.

He ends the letter with the charge to greet the "friends"
(see John 15:15) by name. Imagine how refreshed every disciple would have felt! Imagine how special each brother and
sister would have felt to receive a personal greeting! The apostle
of love, once Son of Thunder and trigger-happy evangelist (Luke
9:54), lets his smile shine through this frank and serious epistle.
He expected the congregation to change. Without change—
constant change—there can be no "life to the full."

? What does the truth speak of your life? Does the truth reveal you to be a person
who sincerely loves God with all his or her heart and loves others deeply from the
heart?

25

Putrescent Religiosity
JUDE

Good things can go bad. Bread goes moldy, apples rot and corpses decompose. The smell of decay is everywhere in the religious world—a clear sign of the death that has occurred. People try to cover up the stench with the smell of candles and incense, but never deal with the real problem. The decay of the "corrupt generation" (Acts 2:40) has invaded Christendom like a hot virus. Can't you smell it? Or are you so used to it that it doesn't bother you anymore?

Jude could not stand it—even when decomposition was just threatening to set in. Check your condition, absorb his conviction and share his compassion.

> *¹Jude, a servant of Jesus Christ and a brother of James,*
> *To those who have been called, who are loved by God the*
> *Father and kept by Jesus Christ:*
> *²Mercy, peace and love be yours in abundance.*

Jude, like the other authors we have studied, wishes his readers the abundant life, life to the full. He is confident that God is always ready to give "in abundance." But there was a problem. The gospel was being perverted; the once-living faith of the church was yielding, in some quarters, to mere "churchianity," or religion without a real relationship with God.

> *³Dear friends, although I was very eager to write to you about the salvation we share, I felt I had to write and urge you to contend for the faith that was once for all entrusted to the saints. ⁴For certain men whose condemnation was written about long ago have secretly slipped in among you. They are godless men, who change the grace of our God into a license for immorality and deny Jesus Christ our only Sovereign and Lord.*

Jude's original intention was to discuss salvation with his readers (verse 3). But the urgent need that had cropped up—lawless men infiltrating the fellowship—altered his agenda. Preachers cannot always follow their notes; sometimes the plan must be scrapped in order to meet the pressing needs of the body of Christ. The looming danger here: cheap grace. And those teaching error are religious men, and worse, they are in the fellowship. Perhaps these were like the "televangelists" of our day—high-flying, Bible-toting, grace-proclaiming hypocrites. Maybe they are self-proclaimed intellectuals, bent on warning the "plebes" of the errors of "fundamentalism" and "fanaticism."

The "faith once for all entrusted to the saints" (verse 3) is more than just a feeling of faith; it is the sum total of Christian belief. As such it must be jealously, zealously guarded. There is no new revelation, since through the apostolic age, the unchangeable foundation of truth was laid. No, in our age there is no revelation, *only* deeper insight into revelation and then application.

These men (verse 4) are the same men Peter warns the church against in 2 Peter 2. The parallels are numerous. Turning God's grace into "a license for immorality" (verse 4) shows that these men were "libertines." The position of the libertine was that, since our sins are going to be forgiven, it doesn't matter how much we sin. Some libertines even argued that the more we sin, the more God's grace is poured out, and thereby the more God's goodness is shown. (Romans 6:1 and following deals with this sort of heresy.)

Every generation has its libertines. Take a good look at the perversions plaguing the modern "church." The sheer number of child abuse cases in the traditional priesthood is staggering. Behold the burgeoning gay clergy. Watch the self-styled prophets of prosperity and popularity. Speak to members of practically any denomination and be astounded at how rampant sin is—and how heartily so-called intellectuals defend it! (See Romans 1:32.)

Jude calls these men "godless." Not that they didn't believe in God or go to church, for they did. They were godless because each of them was his own god. They denied the sovereign lordship of Jesus Christ, preferring the false democracy of their own emancipated opinions.

? What things have you read in the newspaper or heard on the news recently that show that the kind of religion Jude opposed is still with us in our world? Is your opposition to it as strong as was Jude's?

> *⁵Though you already know all this, I want to remind you that the Lord delivered his people out of Egypt, but later destroyed those who did not believe. ⁶And the angels who did not keep their positions of authority but abandoned their own home—these he has kept in darkness, bound with everlasting chains for judgment on the great Day.*

We too must watch our step. As the new covenant people of God, we must learn the lessons taught to the old covenant people of God. Israel exited Egypt, but that did not guarantee they would be saved unconditionally. Even angels, as exalted as their positions apparently were, when they let their position go to their heads, were caught, incarcerated and will ultimately be condemned. Paul reminds us of the example of these evil angelic beings in 1 Corinthians 11, in his discussion on women in church. If even angels could fall through overconfidence, we too must watch ourselves (Christian women in this context).

Notice that, at least from the perspective of time-bound human beings, judgment day has not yet happened (verse 6). Heaven and hell are future, not present, realities.

> *⁷In a similar way, Sodom and Gomorrah and the surrounding towns gave themselves up to sexual immorality and perversion. They serve as an example of those who suffer the punishment of eternal fire.*

Sodom and Gomorrah, doubtless a religious (yet godless) society, were judged in this world for their perversion. The people of God are often reminded of Sodom's ingratitude, rebelliousness, worldliness and sordidness as a sober warning (see Isaiah 1:10; Luke 17:32). The punishment of eternal fire, interestingly, is eternal only in its consequences, its effects, not eternal in its duration. But we cannot go into these matters now.

> *⁸In the very same way, these dreamers pollute their own bodies, reject authority and slander celestial beings. ⁹But even*

the archangel Michael, when he was disputing with the devil
about the body of Moses, did not dare to bring a slanderous
accusation against him, but said, "The Lord rebuke you!" ¹⁰Yet
these men speak abusively against whatever they do not un-
derstand; and what things they do understand by instinct, like
unreasoning animals—these are the very things that destroy
them.

"These men are dreamers" (verse 8) is quite possibly a reference to false visions and oracles, as with the false prophets
in the OT. (Read Jeremiah 23 and see what you think.) There's
no reasoning with these men, no fellowship with them and no
realistic chance of converting them. They are enemies of the
faith, working from within to undermine the work of God.
(Notice the strong parallels to 2 Peter 2.)

Jude 9 refers to a common Jewish tradition about the fate
of the body of Moses, a tradition which Jude seems to accept.
(More on this below in commentary on verse 14.)

The bottom line is that we must be careful. Nations, individuals, angels and societies have fallen into irreparable ruin
because of licentiousness and moral carelessness (verse 4).

¹¹Woe to them! They have taken the way of Cain; they have
rushed for profit into Balaam's error; they have been destroyed
in Korah's rebellion.

It is almost as if these three gentlemen—Cain (Genesis 4),
Balaam (Numbers 22-25) and Korah (Numbers 16)—were the
false teachers' spiritual rolemodels and heroes.

Cain: Their sacrifices were cheap, they became defensive
when challenged, and they were emotionally self-focused instead of repentant. They hated their brothers who were passing them up spiritually.

Balaam: Their secret motives were impure and Mammon
was a chief god in their idolatrous pantheon. You will recall
that on the outside Balaam looked good, going through all the
right motions, yet in his heart he was steered by materialistic
lust.

Korah: These men have serious problems with authority!
Not just parental or civil authority—though doubtless that was
true too—but *spiritual* authority. Negative attitudes towards

church leaders, run-ins with elders and evangelists, seething resentment and an arrogant confidence that "If I were in charge, things would be better."

? What is the difference between a person who has honest questions and a sincere heart and someone who has the spirit of Korah. Perhaps it would help to reread Numbers 16.

> *[12]These men are blemishes at your love feasts, eating with you without the slightest qualm—shepherds who feed only themselves. They are clouds without rain, blown along by the wind; autumn trees, without fruit and uprooted—twice dead. [13]They are wild waves of the sea, foaming up their shame; wandering stars, for whom blackest darkness has been reserved forever.*

The "love feasts" (verse 12) are communion meals. Fellowship suppers dedicated to the memory of Jesus seem to have been the practice in the early church, rather than the traditional ceremonial Lord's Supper observances we are used to.[1] These enemies of the faith joined in without the slightest qualm—a sign that their consciences were cauterized.

Jude calls them "shepherds" (verse 12). This implies that they were leaders, more on the pattern of the bad shepherds of Ezekiel 34 than on the pattern of the Good Shepherd of John 10. These shepherds, like some of the gluttonous Corinthians, fed only themselves (1 Corinthians 11).

Before we express our indignation, are we pointing hypocritical fingers? How about our own hearts? Why are we Christians? Why are we leaders? Does our own appetite (for pleasure, power, acceptance, fame or anything else not worthy of being sought as an end in itself) steer our words, thoughts and actions?

These pseudo-Christians are compared to clouds, trees, waves and stars. Clouds that promise rainfall but instead leave the drought unquenched (Proverbs 25:14). Fruitless trees (autumn, not spring) that will ultimately be cursed and burned (Hebrews 6:7-8). Wild waves, neither tamed nor broken, "foaming up their shame" (verse 13; see also Philippians 3:18-19).

---

[1] However, some commentators believe that eating a meal together may not have been the practice of the early church—one possible implication of 1 Corinthians 11:22.

This brings up immediate images of brazen worldliness: alcoholic froth and rabid revelry. Wandering stars that are independent, egotistical and "legends in their own minds"! In the Bible, stars often stand for angels, but here they represent human beings. Such colorful language, such vivid imagery is more than mere rhetoric or teaching technique. This shows God's deep hatred of sin and the shocking reality of the spiritual condition of these enemies of the cross. Jude, considering its length, is surely the most colorful book in the entire Bible! The spiritual facts are black and white, yet in order to grip and move our hearers we cannot present them in a lackluster manner. We must spare no color as we paint an accurate picture of the spiritual world around us.

> [14]*Enoch, the seventh from Adam, prophesied about these men: "See, the Lord is coming with thousands upon thousands of his holy ones* [15]*to judge everyone, and to convict all the ungodly of all the ungodly acts they have done in the ungodly way, and of all the harsh words ungodly sinners have spoken against him."*

What is this prophecy of Enoch to which Jude refers? And what of the reference to Michael and Moses (verse 9)? Are these works to which he alludes inspired in some way? Verse 14 refers to "Enoch," an apocalyptic Jewish work, originally written in Aramaic in the second century B.C. Enoch belongs to the Pseudepigrapha, so called because of its false authorship. Enoch, as you will recall (Genesis 5), was taken up to heaven without experiencing death and, because of this, was a popular figure in Jewish speculative theology, along with Elijah and Moses.

Enoch promised judgment on the unrighteous which was appropriate for the current situation (licentious faith). The exact reference is 1 Enoch 1:9. It is quite possible that the opponents of the disciples were appealing to Enoch, and Jude was simply using their own weapon against them. Or possibly Jude simply found part of Enoch relevant to his discussion and, knowing that his readers would be familiar with it, did not hesitate to make an ad hoc argument.

Occasional references and allusions do not prove that the author accepted the source work as inspired. In Acts 17, Paul, in his speech on the Areopagus, refers to and quotes from a number of pagan writers and poets. In Titus 1:12 Paul quotes the Cretan writer Epimenides of Knossos. Even the OT's references to the book of Jashar, the Annals of the Kings of Judah and Israel, and many more nonextant works (those unavailable to us) prove nothing per se about the inspiration of those works. Truth is found, in small nuggets, in many places around the world, but in its totally pure, unadulterated form, only in God's word, the Bible.

Even today, many sermons are full of quotations and allusions! The fact that I quote the Beatles does not mean that deep down I feel the Liverpool boys were inspired by God! I merely find the thoughts they expressed helpful in the context of the points I'm trying to make.

Conclusion: the Pseudepigraphal book of Enoch is *not* inspired. It would take a lot more than a single quotation to establish inspiration. In the same way, the reference in verse 9, alluding to something which is unfamiliar to most readers today, tells us nothing about the authority of the total piece to which the citation belongs.

So much for the reference to 1 Enoch. The comforting point is that in no *way* will these men get away with their arrogance. God himself, through angelic hosts, will most assuredly call them to task!

> *16These men are grumblers and faultfinders; they follow their own evil desires; they boast about themselves and flatter others for their own advantage.*
> *17But, dear friends, remember what the apostles of our Lord Jesus Christ foretold. 18They said to you, "In the last times there will be scoffers who will follow their own ungodly desires." 19These are the men who divide you, who follow mere natural instincts and do not have the Spirit.*

"Grumbling and fault-finding" (verse 16) requires no special insight. Anyone can become this way through self-focus, lack of prayer or simply associating with the wrong sorts of characters.

Jude's targets are churchgoing, yet at the same time deeply unspiritual. Their religiosity was putrescent and corrupted! They would claim, no doubt, to have the inside track on the Holy Spirit, but Jude insists this is sheer delusion. Real spirituality is so much more than religion.

? Is there any tendency in you at all to be a grumbler or a fault-finder? Why is God, both in the OT and the NT, so opposed to such an attitude?

> [20]*But you, dear friends, build yourselves up in your most holy faith and pray in the Holy Spirit.* [21]*Keep yourselves in God's love as you wait for the mercy of our Lord Jesus Christ to bring you to eternal life.*

Jude urges us to "pray in the Holy Spirit" (verse 20). Charismatics and others are sure this means "praying in tongues," though there is not a shred of evidence to support this interpretation scripturally. Since the gift of languages was a temporary gift given only to a few, God would only be embittering his children by asking them to do something that only a few have the special ability to do.[2]

So what is praying in the Spirit? It's praying spiritually. It is praying with faith and with dependence on God. It is praying prayers of surrender to the will of God, expressing our real heart, mind, soul and will. It is praying for the world to be evangelized in our generation. Are your prayers spiritual, or would you be embarrassed if your elders were to listen in on your times of prayer?

We are urged to "keep ourselves in God's love" (verse 21). Those who wrongly hold that it is impossible to fall away, or lose one's salvation, point to Romans 8:39, which affirms that nothing can separate us from the love of God. But this magnificent passage never says we cannot of our own volition walk away from the God who loves us. It is our job to keep ourselves in the safe place. (See also Philippians 2:12-13.)

> [22]*Be merciful to those who doubt;* [23]*snatch others from the fire and save them; to others show mercy, mixed with fear— hating even the clothing stained by corrupted flesh.*

"Be merciful to those who doubt" (verse 22). We all go through rough patches, through up times and down times. There is a time for church discipline and even excommunication (1 Corinthians 5:12-13), but towards those who doubt we are commanded to be merciful—not to expel them from the body of Christ.

---

[2]For a more thorough treatment of this subject, see my earlier book, *The Powerful Delusion.*

Just how limited is your patience? Do you really have the mind of Christ in regard to the weak? Do you pass them by in the fellowship? Do you frequently have them into your home? Paul said, "Help the weak" (1 Thessalonians 5:14), not, "Shoot the weak." (Achtung!) These poor souls had been contaminated by the unrighteous influence of the libertines and needed help.

How does clothing become "stained by corrupted flesh" (verse 23)? Perhaps this is a reference to the things that made one unclean under levitical law (Leviticus 11-14). More likely Jude means that we should keep a certain distance between ourselves and the unspiritual, insofar as we might be tempted (Galatians 6:1), No chance should be taken; we want to preserve the pristine purity of the body of Christ. (See also Revelation 3:4.)

> [24]To him who is able to keep you from falling and to present you before his glorious presence without fault and with great joy—[25]to the only God our Savior be glory, majesty, power and authority, through Jesus Christ our Lord, before all ages, now and forevermore! Amen.

Yes, God is able to keep you from falling—falling away—and equally able to present you at the last day joyful and confident in his presence. We will be saved, we will be blameless in God's sight through the blood of Christ our Lord. Amen!

Conclusion

It's amazing what Jude, the brother of Jesus, was able to pack into twenty-five verses! We are thankful for his straight talk. Now may we speak out just as directly, dramatically and devotedly.

Though Jude cried out two millennia ago, his clarion voice still resounds. We have been alerted, the enemy has been identified and solutions have been put forward. There is work to do! Man is still the same, the mission is the same and an unevangelized world lies before us. What are you doing about it?

? What does Jude 24 and 25 mean to you? What about this passage gives you reason to celebrate?

Conclusion

Life to the Full!

L ive and let live, some people say. But how can you live apart from God? You can't! We need him; he is the source of life. Hopefully this theme has emerged loud and clear from our study. The seven general letters by now should not feel so general any more, as the word of God has, prayerfully, come into sharp focus. Have you ever stared into those posters with the hidden 3-D pictures and seen the image suddenly come into clear view? What a surprise the first time it happens! Similarly, it is incredible what the magic eyes of faith can see!

In the same way, it's only by intently looking into the "perfect law that gives freedom" (James 1:25) that the Scriptures come into sharp focus, losing their apparent two-dimensionality and turning out to have (at least) three dynamic dimensions. And as the Scriptures are illuminated, the abundant life God offers suddenly looms into view, then overshadows and at last totally absorbs the man or woman of God. Everything changes, looks different. "Life to the full" becomes reality.

Fantastic! Life to the full: What an offer! Who, after tasting this life, after tasting how good the Lord is, could turn it down? Ah, but many do. Just as the life of the disciple requires discipline, the concentration demanded by mature and intensive Bible study is considerable. Is it really worth it? Ask anyone walking with the Lord, anyone aglow with the Spirit. The answer always comes back: "Absolutely yes!" "When your words came, I ate them" was Jeremiah's free admission (Jeremiah 15:16).

Exploring is magical. Where do we go from here, you ask? On to further responsible study, whether you are a preacher, teacher, or beginner. Love the word of God, lose yourself in it, let it dominate the horizon of your mind and loom larger and larger until, just like being in the front row at the cinema, the divine screen is all you can see. You will be dazzled, thrilled, deeply touched and energized. The Word will totally absorb you—and vice versa! So explore the Word, experiment and be exhilarated!

Life to the full! We have come from death to life, we love life, and we look forward to the crown of life. It seems appropriate to end by quoting the verse which, through the course of the book, we have referred to, John 10:10:

> The thief comes only to steal and kill and destroy. I came that they may have **life**, and have it **abundantly** (New Revised Standard).

> The thief comes only to steal and kill and destroy; I have come that they may have **life**, and have it **to the full** (New International Version).

Appendixes

APPENDIX A

Turbo Bible Study

Yes, you can skip this appendix—but if you want to be a serious student of the Bible, you need the principles we are about to discuss! To rocket your Bible study forward, I recommend that you:

1. Purchase or borrow some scholarly Bible introductions and commentaries.
2. Read the Bible in several different versions. English has over a hundred, many of which are reasonably accurate.
3. If you are fluent in another language, read through at least the NT in that language.
4. Study once through the OT Apocrypha.
5. Study the writings of the second-century Christian leaders (the "Patristic" writings).
6. Strive to read through the entire Bible regularly. Those in leadership positions should probably aim to do this once annually.

Terminology

Particularly if you want to go on to more advanced reading on the letters, you will have to become familiar with the terminology of NT scholarship. The jargon is considerable! All the NT documents have special names, and to be able to understand any intermediate or advanced work, nomenclature is vital. Here is a sampling of terms to know, all of which relate to study of the general letters:

- Pauline epistles: Belonging to the family of letters written or influenced by Paul
- Pastoral epistles: Describes Paul's letters to Timothy and Titus

- Petrine epistles: Peter's writings
- Jacobine epistle: The letter of James, brother of the Lord—
                         a rather rare term
- Catholic epistles: The general letters of James, Peter, John
                         and Jude
- Hermeneutics: The science of interpretation
- Exegesis: Drawing the meaning out of the text,
                         according to sound historical and
                         literary principles
- Eisegesis: Opposite of the above; reading your
                         preconceived ideas into the text
- Soteriology: The study of salvation and associated
                         doctrines
- Ecclesiology: The study of the church

   The letters of the New Testament are arranged by author,
length and audience. For example, Paul's letters are arranged
into two categories: letters to churches and letters to individuals, each grouping in descending order of length.
   Who arranged them the way our Bibles have them is irrelevant. Some early manuscripts contain the NT books in a different order: Hebrews may follow Romans, Mark can be the
first gospel. Knowing the system will enable you to see where
the letters of James, Peter, John and Jude fit into the scheme of
things. Here, then, is the arrangement of the NT letters, which
number, as Luke might have said, "about 30":

Pauline Epistles

1) Letters to Churches (Romans through 2 Thessalonians)
2) Letters to Individuals
        a) Pastoral epistles (1 Timothy, 2 Timothy, Titus)
        b) Philemon
3) Hebrews (Pauline but not by Paul)

General Epistles [1]

1) James
2) Petrine epistles (1- and 2 Peter)

---

[1] Interestingly, in some of the earliest surviving manuscripts we see the General Letters placed immediately after Acts. The order of the books in the Bible is obviously of
secondary importance, however, and few scholars object to the present order of the
NT books.

3) Johannine epistles (1- through 3 John)
4) Jude

Other Letters

1) Acts 15, letter from Jerusalem Council
2) Revelation 2-3, seven letters to churches in "Asia" (western Turkey). Author: Jesus.
3) Extracanonical letters (see 1 Corinthians 5:9; Colossians 4:16; etc.)

How to Read an Epistle

To begin with, it's recommended you get a good translation. We rely on accurate translations, since the letters are written in Greek, as was the rest of NT. Just for fun, imagine you're reading a letter in the original *koine* Greek. Texts were in all upper or lower case, usually with no spaces between words and no punctuation, either:

σπουδασονσεαυτονδοκιμονπαραστη	canyoustilleasilyreadwhatisbeingsaidev
σαιτωθεωεργατηνανεπαισχυντονορ	enthoughallthespaceshavebeeneliminat
θοτομουντατονλογοντηςαληθειας	edbecauseifyoucanyouareacleverperson

What about chapters and verses? Don't make too much of them, since they were added only in last few centuries. The originals, like letters we write today, lacked chapter and verse divisions. These have been added for our convenience. (No, the numbers are *not* inspired!)

Remember, *you are reading someone else's mail*; it's like hearing only one side of a conversation. 1 Corinthians provides perhaps the clearest illustration of this reality. Verses 1:11, 5:1, 7:1, 7:25, 12:1, 15:1, 16:1, 16:12, 16:19 show that there is a dialogue going on, and that Paul has been informed through "Chloe's people" as well as through the letter from the Corinthians to him.

In fact 1 Corinthians 5:9 mentions a previous letter. Since 2 Corinthians also mentions an earlier letter which, from the context, cannot be 1 Corinthians, it follows that Paul wrote no fewer than four letters to the Corinthians. Is this surprising, considering how long he spent in Corinth (Acts 18)? Similarly, it is possible (I would say almost certain) that James, Peter and others wrote letters which have not survived. It is doubtful they will ever turn up, but even if they were, we can be sure that no new doctrine would be unearthed! The NT is sufficient—this is the historical conviction of the Christian church.

Further Suggestions

- Ask questions: *Who* is writing to *whom? When? Why? What* are the circumstances? *How* are certain terms being used? Ask what is binding: whether specific *advice* or only a *principle,* e.g. Romans 16:16.
- Read slowly and carefully. Other parts of the Bible can be read rapidly but not the letters. (Their inspiration and insight per verse density is very high indeed.)
- Make sure you understand OT citations. Look them up if you are confused, and even if you don't resolve your question, keep it in mind for future study.
- From time to time *pray* through an epistle, reading a verse or two and praying about what comes to your mind, then reading a little further and continuing to draw your inspiration from the text. Read a minute or so, pray a minute or so, alternating till you have finished your selection.
- Read in context: As said before, "A proof text out of context is a pretext."

Summary

Effective Bible study is work. A solid Bible knowledge takes years of practice. There are no shortcuts, but there are loads of study aids, helpful hints and a plethora of ideas to stimulate your cortex.

Finally, 2 Timothy 2:15, written to a Christian evangelist (the verse in Greek you saw above), has something in it for all of us, and for all who aspire to leadership in the kingdom of God:

> *Do your best to present yourself to God as one approved, a workman who does not need to be ashamed and who correctly handles the word of truth.*

APPENDIX B

Apostles and Apostolicity

This appendix will provide extremely valuable background for future study, as well as better equip the disciple to answer common questions posed by outsiders. Because of God's incredible plan in the first century, as we shall see, we are able to stand squarely on the apostolic foundation and so evangelize the world, using their convicting words and going forth in their heroic spirit.

Of the writers of the General Letters only Peter and John are explicitly called "apostles," although the apostolic connection of James and Jude (with Jesus) is loud and clear.

Apostleship

The word "apostle" comes from the Greek *apostolos*, which means "one sent, a missionary." All the apostles were chosen specially by the Lord (Mark 3:13-14; Galatians 1:15). It is helpful to distinguish between two senses of the word apostle:
- Apostle (capital 'A'): One of the thirteen (including Paul); chosen envoys of Jesus
- apostle (small 'a'): a missionary

This distinction clarifies verses like Acts 14:4, 14 (Barnabas) and Romans 16:7 (Junias, a woman). A parallel is found in "Disciple" and "disciple," where all Christians are disciples but sometimes we use the technical term "The Disciples" to refer to Jesus' chosen Twelve.

Eyewitnesses

The Apostles ("capital 'A'") were eyewitnesses (2 Peter 1:16), who had seen Jesus in the flesh (1 John 1:1; 1 Corinthians 9:1; Acts 1:22). One reason is that they had to be able to recognize him *after* his death and resurrection. Hence, contrary to Mormon teaching, there are no apostles today.

Miraculous Endowment

The apostles had miraculous powers before Pentecost (Luke 9:1) and after Pentecost (Acts 2:43). As far as we can be sure, every NT miracle not done by Jesus was done either by an apostle or by someone on whom the apostles had laid their hands. They had the ability to transmit *miraculous* spiritual gifts (Acts 6:6, 6:8, 8:6, 8:18; Romans 1:11). Thus when the last apostle died, the gift of being able to transmit a gift also died: the miraculous apostolic age came to an end.

Writings

The apostles or those closely connected to them wrote four gospels, numerous canonical letters and one book of prophecy (Revelation 1:3). God selected some of their writings, preserved them by his providence and brought them together gradually to form the NT.

Inspiration

Jesus had promised the apostles that through the Spirit his teachings would come to them in an accurate way. (John 14:26 and 16:13 are two excellent memory verses.) Sometimes we call these men "inspired apostles." More accurately, their writings which appear in the NT are inspired.

Infallibility

They were certainly not infallible in their lives (Galatians 2:11), only in their doctrine, insofar as God entrusted them with the task of penning the NT scriptures. As for their inspiration and authority, the church was devoted to *their* teaching (Acts 2:42). That is why they were the foundation of the church (Ephesians 2:20). Obviously, once laid, there was no further need for any new foundation. Hence the apostolic age (with revelation and transmission of miraculous spiritual gifts) is long past.

Apostolicity and the NT

The question is often asked, "How did the Bible come together? Who voted on the books we have?" You may recall that the entire OT was completed more than four centuries before the birth of Christ, and all three divisions of the OT are upheld and cited frequently in the NT (Luke 24:44). Jesus, Paul and other figures of authority believed in and based their arguments on the validity of the OT scriptures.

As for the NT, there was no "vote"! Christians recognized the authority of the apostles, and unless a document had a clear apostolic connection, it was rejected. Of course it took time for letters geographically separated to come together, yet no later than the late second century lists of NT books were coming together, and the present order was firmly established by the fourth century. Did this pose a problem for those with access to only a handful of gospels and letters? Not at all—you could still follow and preach the gospel even with a partial NT. (Do *you* use every NT document when you study the Bible with a friend to teach him the gospel?)

The church councils that met in later centuries did discuss the canon (the official list of accepted books), but it should be recognized that this was in order to *exclude* heretical or non-apostolic writings, not to decide on which apostolic books to *include*. Many pretenders and spurious works were circulating by the third and fourth centuries!

So they key to a NT document belonging in the NT is its "apostolicity," or apostolic connection and authority. (And "apostolicity" is a great word to throw around at parties and impress your friends with!)

The following table demonstrates the fact that every document of the NT has an apostolic connection. Thus writings in subsequent centuries were rightly rejected, since they lacked this connection.

APOSTOLIC CONNECTIONS

Document	Connection	Comments
Matthew	Apostle	One of the original Twelve
Mark	Peter	Heard Peter in Rome; first gospel (45-65 A.D.)
Luke	Paul	Traveling companion of Paul (Acts)

Document	Connection	Comments
John	Apostle	Either earliest or latest gospel
Acts	Paul	Volume 2 of Luke (Acts 1:3)
Romans-Philemon	Apostle	Paul: written in 20 years (48-68 A.D.)
Hebrews	Paul	Clearly someone in Paul's circle (possibly Apollos or Barnabas)
James	Apostle	Brother of Jesus (Galatians 1:19), died 62 A.D.
1 Peter	Apostle	Written late in reign of Nero (54-68 A.D.)
2 Peter	Apostle	Accepts Paul's inspiration (3:16)
1 John	Apostle	Possibly as early as 50s-60s A.D. or as late as 90s
2-3 John	Apostle	The "elder" is probably John himself
Jude	Jesus	A brother of Jesus (Matthew 13:55)
Revelation	Apostle	John, 69-79 A.D.

The Apostles' Epistles

No, an "epistle" is not an apostle's wife! The word "epistle" simply means "letter," from the Latin *epistula*. After planting a church, letters were the best means of keeping in touch, apart from an actual visit. No doubt the early Christians wrote hundreds of letters, most of which have not survived.

As we have seen, unless there was an apostolic connection, the gospel, acts, letter or apocalypse was a forgery. As for the dating of NT documents, while there is room for opinion, most conservative scholars agree on the broad outlines.

In the 1800s, many liberal professors dated the NT documents to the period 100-150 A.D., denying apostolic authorship of *any* of the letters or other documents! Yet as earlier and earlier manuscripts (MSS) have been discovered, the NT has been dated much earlier. Many conservative scholars date the completion of the NT at 96 A.D. Others believe that the bulk, if not the entirety, of the NT was written by the time of the destruction of Jerusalem, 70 A.D.

If we go with the 70 A.D. date, then the NT may have been written in as short a span as twenty years, thirty years tops. In this period (33-70 A.D.), many eyewitnesses to the facts about Jesus were still alive (1 Corinthians 15:6). In other words, my position is that *the NT was written in the first generation of*

Christianity. While we cannot speak with absolute certainty on these matters, the following table gives approximate dates for the NT documents.

Dating of NT Documents

Epistle	Date	Comment
Galatians	48 A.D.	Probably the earliest letter
Mark	50 A.D.	Source for Matthew and Luke
John	50 A.D.	Some scholars date it late, others early
1-2 Thessalonians	50 A.D.	Supported by *Gallio inscription,* Acts 18
James	50 A.D.	Reflects early Jewish Christianity
Romans	55 A.D.	Paul not yet in Rome
Matthew	55 A.D.	The most Jewish of all gospels
1 Corinthians	56 A.D.	Paul's second letter to them (see 5:9)
2 Corinthians	57 A.D.	Paul's fourth (see 7:8—not 1 Corinthians)
Luke - Acts	60 A.D.	Ends with statutory release after two years
Eph, Col, Phm	60 A.D.	These three were written at the same time.
Philippians	61 A.D.	Written from prison
1-2 Peter, Jude	64 A.D.	Killed by Nero, according to 1 Clem, 96 A.D.
1 Timothy	65 A.D.	Written after Paul's release
Titus	66 A.D.	To evangelist on Crete
Hebrews	67 A.D.	To Jewish Christian community
2 Timothy, 1-3 John	68 A.D.	Shortly before Peter's death
Revelation	70 A.D.	See Revelation 17:11.

Support for Early Dating

The last book of the NT is Revelation. Just as the future (not the present) had been revealed to Daniel, so also it was revealed to John. He wrote about, but did not live in, the oppressive days of Domitian, the persecuting emperor who conducted himself towards the disciples in the spirit of Nero.

Revelation 17 would seem to support the idea that John received his revelation in the days of Vespasian. (See Appendix C.) So if the temple that John is to measure is still standing (Revelation 11:1), and refers to the Jerusalem temple, the vision must have come in 69 or 70 A.D. If Herod's Temple has been destroyed, or if temple in Revelation refers to the church of God (as according to Jim McGuiggan, *Revelation,* Star Bible Publications), then Revelation would have been written between 70 and 79 A.D. In support of this view, in Ezekiel the temple is described prophetically even though it has already been destroyed. So it's possible that Revelation was penned between the destruction of Jerusalem (spring 70 A.D.) and 79 A.D. The latest possible date is 79 A.D., the final year of this "fifth king" (Revelation 17:10). It certainly makes things tidy if Revelation were written by the time of the destruction of Jerusalem, but the evidence is not 100% conclusive for the pre-70 A.D. date.

NT Apocrypha

The NT Apocrypha is not to be confused with the OT Apocrypha (Tobit, Judith, 1-2 Maccabees, Ecclesiasticus, Wisdom of Solomon, and additions to Daniel, Esther and Jeremiah, all written in the period "between the testaments"). These writings are typical of the literature rightly excluded from the NT canon. For example, many spurious letters written much later than apostolic times (third-fourth century) and palmed off as apostolic. They contradict biblical teachings, contain many historical errors and are often as sensationalistic, as is much of the cheap literature in religious bookstores today. Some of the legends in the apocrypha even found their way into the Koran, and they were uncritically accepted by the medieval Catholic church.

It is true that other letters were written by the apostles (for instance, 1 Corinthians 5:9; 2 Corinthians 7:8; Colossians 4:16), but none of these has ever been located. What if more letters came to light? That is an interesting prospect, but it's doubtful there would be any new teaching were such writings to be discovered. Unfortunately, pretenders took advantage of the gullible as they made up their doctrine (2 Peter 2:1-3)—yet the persevering people of God always recognized the truth.

God protected his word, and would-be books of the Bible had no more chance of entering the canon than Adam and Eve had of getting back into Eden! The flaming sword of truth saw to that.[2]

---

[2] For a helpful introduction to the issues involved in inspiration and canonization, see Neil R. Lightfoot, *How We Got the Bible* (Grand Rapids: Baker Book House), 1988.

Summary

The NT, including the epistles, was written in the first generation of Christianity—not the third or fourth, as liberal scholars used to maintain. The key criterion for a document to be recognized as inspired and authoritative was apostolicity, an apostolic connection, in fulfillment of the promise made by Jesus to his chosen apostles (John 14:12, 16:13). This includes the general letters of James, Peter, John and Jude: all of them are apostolic. There are no apostles today; the apostolic foundation of the church has been laid once-for-all.

APPENDIX C

Ten Caesars

The following is a listing of the first ten caesars. Technically, the caesars continued well into the fourth century, but these ten are not only the most interesting (in my opinion), but also those of most relevance to NT studies. Getting to know their names by heart, along with their years of office, is a good way to begin orienting oneself with first-century contemporary secular history. The list does not start with Julius Caesar, since he was never emperor, rather dictator—and only for a short time at that. (This is the consensus view of Roman historians and classicists, and theologians.)

This table is included not only for general knowledge of the NT world, but also because it is key in understanding Revelation 17, which allows us to pinpoint the writing of John's prophecy to the fourth decade after Christ, thus strongly demonstrating that the NT was written in the first generation of Christianity.

Ten Caesars

Roman Emperors	Dates	Events
1. Augustus Caesar	27 B.C.-14 A.D.	Jesus born, 5 B.C.
2. Tiberius Caesar	14-37 A.D.	Jesus' ministry (28-31 A.D.) & death (31 A.D.)
3. Caligula Caesar	37-41	Mad emperor
4. Claudius Caesar	41-54	Expelled Jews from Rome (Acts 18)
5. Nero Caesar	54-68	Blamed Christians for fire of 64; torture; martyrdoms of Peter (64) and Paul (68)
[Galba-Otho-Vitellius]	69	Unsuccessful attempts to be emperor
6. Vespasian Caesar	69-79	Started siege of Jerusalem (Matthew 24)
7. Titus Caesar	79-81	Finished siege (70), short reign

Roman Emperors	Dates	Events
8. Domitian Caesar	81-96	Empire-wide persecution, setting of Revelation; claimed divinity in his lifetime
9. Nerva	96-98	Had a lot of nerve
10. Trajan	98-117	Illegal to be a Christian